The California Angels

by Ross Newhan

Editor of Baseball Series:
Gene Schoor

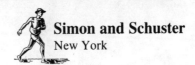

Simon and Schuster
New York

Copyright © 1982 by Gene Schoor
All rights reserved
including the right of reproduction
in whole or in part in any form
Published by Simon and Schuster
A Division of Gulf & Western Corporation
Simon & Schuster Building
Rockefeller Center
1230 Avenue of the Americas
New York, New York 10020

SIMON AND SCHUSTER and colophon are
trademarks of Simon & Schuster
Designed by Irving Perkins Associates
Manufactured in the United States of America
10 9 8 7 6 5 4 3 2 1

Library of Congress Cataloging in Publication Data

Newhan, Ross.
  The California Angels.
  1. Angels (Baseball team)—History. I. Title.
GV875.A6N48   796.357′64′0979494   82-700
ISBN 0-671-42059-3   AACR2

Acknowledgments

The author wishes to thank all those who aided in the preparation of this work. I particularly wish to thank Tom Seeburg, director of public relations for the Angels, and my wife, Connie, for her help and understanding, and to give a very special acknowledgment to my dad, Leonard, and mother, Bertha, for keeping a daily scrapbook of my Angel stories for more than twenty years.

My gratitude also goes to my great editor at Simon and Schuster, Peter Schwed, for his aid and comfort, and to Julian Bach, my agent, who helped develop this great series of baseball books.

For my Father and Mother
And with all my love
to
Connie, Sara and David

Chapter

1

HE MADE 95 movies and more than 125 records. He hosted a national radio show. He toured the country, appearing in concerts and rodeos.

Now, at 72 and long-since retired as an entertainer, Gene Autry, the singing cowboy, a cinematic hero in an age of heroes, was back in the spotlight—back in the saddle, so to speak. He was pursued by men holding notebooks and microphones. His reactions were captured by the television cameras. He might have responded favorably to a request for a song had there been one, in his present joyful mood.

It was the night of September 25, 1979. The Anaheim Stadium clubhouse of the California Angels, Autry's Angels, now champions of the American League's Western Division after a just-completed 4–1 victory over the former champions, the Kansas City Royals.

While many in the crowd of 40,361 poured onto the field to stage the type of celebration that has become familiar after such clinchings, Autry and a colleague, a former President of the United States named Richard Nixon, walked to an elevator that would carry them to a clubhouse already awash in champagne.

For the Angels, however, the celebration was anything but familiar.

This was the first championship in the 19-year history of a franchise awarded to Autry in 1961. It had come to him through a series of ironies, the culmination of a lifelong love of the game, a romance that began in Tioga, Texas, where Orvon Gene Autry was born on September 29, 1907, the place where he first swung a bat and strummed a guitar.

The guitar was purchased for $8 through a Sears Roebuck catalogue. The 12-year-old Autry had earned the money by baling and stacking hay on his Uncle Calvin's farm. Autry was always cognizant of the value of money because there was so little of it then. His mother died when she was 45 because she had been unable to afford the proper medical care. His father drifted off soon after that, a self-styled merchant and trader who, on most days, found business more difficult to cultivate than that arid land.

Autry was 15 when he went to work as a baggage smasher and was then promoted to a job for $35 a month as a telegrapher on the Frisco Line, a position he still held at 19 when, while picking at his guitar to kill time during a four-to-midnight shift in Chelsea, Oklahoma, a visitor to the office asked him to keep at it while he prepared some copy for Autry to send. The enthusiastic Autry began to sing, finishing at about the time that the visitor finished his copy. The man said, "You know, with some hard work, young man, you might have something. You ought to think about going to New York and get yourself a job on radio."

The visitor's name was Will Rogers, who never met a man he didn't like and was among the first to express an appreciation for Autry's musical ability, a measure of encouragement that would ultimately send Autry, whose mother played the guitar and organ at church and family functions but who envisioned her son becoming a professional man, in search of a show business career.

The remarkable events that followed might never have occurred had Rogers not been visiting his sister in Chelsea that summer, and had the St. Louis Cardinals offered more than $100 a month to Autry when he tried out with their Tulsa farm club as a 19-year-old-shortstop who had gained experience playing with Tioga's American Legion team. The scouting report on the guitar player was that he was a banjo hitter who could make all the fielding plays. There were no big bonuses then, no multiyear contracts of the type that an owner named Autry would ultimately give out, and he decided to reject the St. Louis offer in favor of retaining his now $150-a-month job with the railroad.

The dream of playing, however, didn't die easily. Baseball was truly the national pastime then, a national avenue of escape, particularly for youths born to poverty. The game remained Autry's passion, nurtured by the success of boyhood friend Dizzy Dean, during his own success in other entertainment arenas. He attended games whenever he could. He became friends with owners and players, the athletes as anxious to meet him as he was to meet them. He scheduled the World's Championship Rodeo into Madison Square Garden each October in the hope that one of the New York teams would be in the World Series.

The telegrapher from Tioga, the singing cowboy, the man who made Rudolph more famous than Dasher and Dancer, and who always rode Champion on a trail of law and order, would become an entertainment and corporate legend, a multimillionaire. But with baseball, both before and after 1961, he would always be just a fan, a boy of summer, an owner who writes a letter of appreciation to just about every player who leaves his organization, and who has made innumerable trips to the clubhouse to visit with his players, to sit on a stool and reminisce, particularly with those who were from a time when batting and earned run averages were more important than the Dow Jones, when the instruction given by managers and coaches was more important than that given by agents and attorneys.

"I imagine," said Nolan Ryan, one of Autry's most celebrated pitchers, standing by his locker as he watched the champagne-soaked owner move through the champagne-soaked clubhouse on that September night in 1979, "he's 'bout as happy right now as he can remember being."

"Yes We Can," the Angels' theme in 1979, had just become "Yes We Did." The headline in the *Los Angeles Times* the next morning would read, "Autry Finally Has Another Champion." And the owner would tell the men holding notebooks and microphones that, yes, he was 'bout as happy as he could remember being, his happiness intensified by the fact that while his 19 years as an owner had been among his most exciting, they were also among his most frustrating.

Only five times in the previous 18 years had the Angels finished at or above .500. Only once had they finished higher than third. There had been 1,598 losses to go with 1,464 wins, and Autry had invested more than $20 million while employing 8 managers, 4 general managers and more than 350 players.

In addition, the franchise seemed cursed by a hex, a jinx, a spell. The players avoided talking about it, but there were constant reminders. It started right from the beginning. It started in 1961, when the American League expanded to Los Angeles and Washington, D.C.

The Angels acquired a promising pitcher named Johnny James from the Yankees early that year. James was in his 37th game as an Angel when he threw a curve ball and felt something snap. It was a bone in his arm. He never pitched again.

In April of 1962, after hitting 25 home runs the previous year, outfielder Ken Hunt, waiting in the on-deck circle, flexed his back by arching a bat behind his head. Hunt, too, heard something snap. He had broken his collarbone. He never played a full season again.

In August of that year, with the sophomore Angels making an improbable run at the pennant, Art Fowler, their best relief pitcher, was lost for the final six weeks when hit by a line drive during batting practice in Boston. Fowler lost the vision in his left eye and was never the same pitcher.

In the spring of 1964, Ken McBride, the ace of the early pitching staffs, a winner of ten straight games at one point, suffered neck and back injuries in a car accident and won only four more games in his career.

In the summer of 1964, Autry gave $300,000 in signing bonuses to outfielder Rick Reichardt and catcher Tom Egan. The former, a coveted power hitter from the University of Wisconsin, soon started to experience severe headaches. Medical tests disclosed a blood disorder, and Reichardt was forced to have a kidney removed. The once bright potential was never fulfilled, and Reichardt played out his career as a journeyman. Egan, a widely sought southern California high school player, eventually became the Angels' No. 1 catcher. He was beaned by Detroit's Earl Wilson in 1969, suffered a broken jaw, and never regained complete sight in his left eye.

In 1965, rookie Dick Wantz pitched impressively in spring training and was a surprise addition to the varsity staff. He seemed headed for stardom. Within four months, he was dead, the victim of a brain tumor at 25.

In April of 1968, first baseman Don Mincher, 25 homers and 78 runs batted in the year before, was beaned by Cleveland's Sam McDowell. His career was finished. In June of the same year, third baseman Paul Schaal had his jaw fractured when struck by a pitch thrown by Boston's Jose Santiago. He was soon traded, never to be the same hitter.

In the winter of 1968, Minnie Rojas, a brilliant and tireless relief pitcher for three straight years, was involved in a car accident near his Miami home. Rojas' wife and two of three children were killed. Rojas was permanently paralyzed.

In the winter of 1972, utility infielder Chico Ruiz was killed in a car accident near his San Diego home. He was 33.

On May 17, 1973, infielder-outfielder Bobby Valentine, a charismatic and talented young player, broke his leg so severely when he crashed into the center field fence while chasing a fly ball at Anaheim Stadium that he never played on a regular basis again.

In the spring of 1974, rookie Bruce Heinbechner, 23, expected to be the club's left-handed relief specialist, was killed in an auto accident about a half mile from the team's Palm Springs hotel.

In the summer of 1975, pitcher Jim McGlothlin, 33, a consistent winner during five years with the Angels, died of cancer.

In the winter of 1977, shortstop Mike Miley, 23, an expected starter with the Angels, was killed in a Louisiana auto accident.

In the summer of 1977, outfielder Joe Rudi and second baseman Bobby Grich, two free agents for whom Autry paid $2 million and $1.5 million, respectively, were lost for the majority of the season with injuries. Rudi broke a wrist and Grich suffered a herniated disc.

In September of 1978, outfielder Lyman Bostock, a $2.2 million free agent, was shot fatally while riding in a car with family and friends in Gary, Indiana. He was 27.

There were aspects of the hoodoo also in 1979, even as the Angels were winning the West. Manager Jim Fregosi was forced to use 81 different lineups to compensate for 47 injuries. That, and what had come before, tended to make this first title all the sweeter for Autry and his manager, one of the club's original draft choices and the starting shortstop for almost a decade. Fregosi would sit in his office long after the final cork had popped and say that the thing he would always remember about that night was the look in Autry's eyes, the expression on his face.

But if Autry believed the frustration was finally behind him, bathed away by the champagne, by the consummation of his quest for a title, he soon learned otherwise. The radiance of late evening was gone before the first light of morning.

Pitcher Jim Barr broke his right hand during a victory party altercation at a nearby restaurant and was unable to work in the championship series against Baltimore, the Orioles capturing the American League pennant in four games.

And a year later, with his club favored to repeat in the West, Autry watched with shock and disbelief as the Angels succumbed to their worst injury wave ever, falling far behind in a race in which they were never a factor. Among others, in June of 1980, pitcher Bruce Kison, a $2.4 million free agent, underwent wrist and elbow surgery and was lost for the season, winning only three games.

It was more of the same in 1981 when the season was split in two by a strike of the Major League Players Association and the touted Angels finished far back in both races. In the summer of 1981, center fielder Fred Lynn, a former American League Most Valuable Player who had been acquired from Boston in a major winter trade and signed to a 4-year, $5.3 million contract, injured his left knee and batted just .219, or 89 points below his career average. Pitcher Bill Travers, signed to a 5-year, $1.5 million free agent contract, developed tendinitis in the spring and pitched only 9⅔ innings all year.

Chapter

II

PAT BUTTRAM, Gene Autry's comic sidekick on radio and television, likes to say of Autry that "He used to ride off into the sunset. Now he owns it." Buttram also says of Autry, "He can't sing and he can't act, but he sure can count."

When Buttram isn't repeating those lines, Autry is, adding that he'd say to Buttram, "I know I can't act but what the hell is my judgment against that of 50 million fans?"

Gene Autry has always considered himself more a personality than actor, more a storyteller than singer. He sold 40 million records. "Rudolph the Red-Nosed Reindeer" alone sold 10 million. Autry had initially rejected it as being silly. His late wife, Ina Mae, insisted he record it, saying it reminded her of the story of the Ugly Duckling and that "the kids will love it."

She was right. Kids from 8 to 80 adored the song. Rudolph's success moved Autry out of the country class and to the top of the pop charts for the first time. It was his single biggest success in an entertainment career that earned him approximately $5 million. He has earned many times that much as a corporate cowboy, traveling an avenue made accessible to him because of the money he made as an entertainer.

"Whatever I own, whatever I have accomplished," Autry once said, "didn't happen by chance. Even as a boy I planned ahead. When I was a baggage smasher at 15 for the Frisco Railroad, and later a telegrapher, I still took correspondence courses and became an accountant. There has always been a kind of linkage in my life."

There has also always been the touch of Midas, an innate sense of when and how to move on.

"Johnny Bond, who toured and worked with me on radio, once told me about an Old West tradition," Autry says. "Whenever an Indian or lone cowboy had to take a long trip, he would generally ride one saddled horse and lead another bareback. When his horse began to tire, he didn't have to stop for a rest. He simply slipped the saddle onto the spare horse and continued on. I kind of went from performer to businessman in the same way. I kind of just changed horses."

The cornerstone of Autry's empire is Golden West Broadcasters, whose umbrella shelters AM radio stations in Los Angeles and San Francisco, AM-FM affiliates in Portland, Seattle and Detroit, a UHF station in Oklahoma City, subscription and cable TV outlets in Memphis, Omaha, Dallas, Providence, Chicago and Atlanta, a Los Angeles TV channel, a ten-acre movie and TV production center, a national agency for selling radio time, and a baseball team called the California Angels.

Autry privately owns a Palm Springs hotel (he formerly owned several others, including the Mark Hopkins in San Francisco), a television station in Phoenix, a 20,000-acre cattle ranch in Winslow, Arizona, four recording and music publishing companies and the 100-acre Melody Ranch in Newhall, California, where Autry made his first starring movies some 45 years ago.

In a career that has spanned two spheres renowned for their often cutthroat methods, Autry has never been known as the kind of person who attained the summit by climbing over the bodies of those who failed.

They tell the story in Hollywood about the time Autry was

staging a salary strike at Republic Studio, which, while conducting a publicity campaign designed to promote Roy Rogers, was ready to sweep Rogers out when Autry returned. Autry reportedly refused to let the studio do that, demanding it continue the buildup for the young cowboy who would soon become his chief competitor.

The late Herb Green, Autry's personal pilot for 30 years, remembered Autry taking his show to a theater in Milwaukee for a week. It was during a polio epidemic and the house was empty, creating panic for the theater owner, who had a contract with Autry and could see himself going broke.

"At the end of the week," Green said, "Gene tore up the contract and took the loss out of his own pocket. He's that kind of guy. He's a giver. But try to cheat him out of a dollar and he'll fight you like a grizzly."

Shrewd, determined, self-educated and gifted with unique instincts, Autry changed horses and prospered, making only one illogical investment—he has frequently said, suppressing a smile. That, of course, was his purchase of a baseball team, a step that might not have been taken if the late Walter O'Malley, who moved his Dodgers from Brooklyn to Los Angeles in 1958, had kept the game broadcasts on Autry's radio station (KMPC) rather than moving them to another (KFI). It was a step that also might not have been taken if Autry had not once done a favor for the then American League president, Joe Cronin, and if the Japanese had not bombed Pearl Harbor on December 7, 1941.

Autry does not require his accountant's training to read a ledger sheet that shows the Angels suffering an operating loss in 12 of the 20 years. Some of that loss has been used advantageously from a tax standpoint. All of it has been covered by the immense advertising profits generated by KMPC's broadcasts of the games. Yet, Autry is fond of saying, "If you lose $500,000, you lose $500,000, no matter what."

And Autry is painfully aware that if it hadn't been for the $2.5 million profit in 1979, when the club won its first title and drew 2,523,575 at Anaheim Stadium, the bottom line on 20 years would be written in red.

People pursue sports franchises for varied and complicated reasons. Tax shelter. Lifetime dream. Ego trip. Autry made his move after O'Malley made one of his own, purchasing a summer home in the San Gabriel Mountains above Los Angeles.

It was the summer of 1960 and O'Malley would later inform Autry that on nights when the Dodgers were on the road he was unable to pick up KMPC's signal at his mountain retreat. O'Malley offered the explanation only after Autry had read about the Dodgers' decision to switch stations in *Variety,* the show business newspaper.

"I was shocked," Autry said. "Bob Reynolds, my partner, and Stan Spero, my general manager at KMPC, had personally negotiated with O'Malley and believed they had his word on a contract renewal. We had spent all kinds of money in supporting his fight to build in Chavez Ravine. It was hard to believe. The ironic thing is that the Dodgers ultimately ended up on a station whose nighttime power is so weak you have trouble picking up the games even in Orange County. I guess those things have a way of evening up."

O'Malley, at that point, had been in Los Angeles for three years, his team meeting with a popularity and success that even a visionary such as himself could not have predicted. The West Coast became the Gold Coast, and the American League became keenly interested in doing its own mining.

On October 26, 1960, at a New York meeting, the league voted owner Calvin Griffith permission to move his Washington Senators to Minneapolis–St. Paul and also voted to expand to 10 teams in 1961, creating franchises in Los Angeles and Washington, D.C.

Hank Greenberg, a Hall of Fame hitter who was a part owner of the Chicago White Sox, was asked by the league to take over the Los Angeles club, and Greenberg indicated he hoped to form a syndicate that would include San Diego banker C. Arnholt Smith, ex-major leaguer Ralph Kiner and the flamboyant Bill Veeck, then a Greenberg partner in the White Sox.

Autry, at the time having lost the Dodgers to KFI, was more interested in acquiring a client than a franchise. He wanted to retain KMPC's reputation as southern California's sports station, and he knew it would be difficult if both the Dodgers and the new American League team were on other channels. Autry quickly made arrangements to meet with Greenberg and Veeck on one of their trips to Los Angeles, and they agreed to have KMPC broadcast the games if their deal with the league went through.

It did not. The obstacle was O'Malley, who argued that existing rules did not permit the American League to move into his territory, and he was supported by then Commissioner Ford Frick. The problem really seemed to be one of personality and money. Greenberg and Veeck were not interested in meeting O'Malley's demand for $450,000 in indemnification, and O'Malley, not anxious to share his chunk of the Gold Coast with anyone, was particularly not anxious to do it with a magnetic showman such as Veeck.

Amid the threat of a war between the two leagues, the American League met in New York again on November 17; awarded the Washington franchise to a syndicate headed by Lieutenant General Elwood R. (Pete) Quesada, a World War II hero and chairman of the Federal Aviation Agency; agreed on a course of action for amending the expansion rules O'Malley had cited; and accepted Greenberg's withdrawal from the Los Angeles picture. The new bidder became a Gary, Indiana, insurance man named Charles Finley.

Meanwhile, back at Melody Ranch, Autry and partner Robert Reynolds, with the urging of a friend, construction magnate and Yankee co-owner Del Webb, were now considering the possibility of bidding themselves. Reynolds, a strapping six-foot-four piece of steel who was an All-American tackle at Stanford and the only man ever to play three 60-minute games in the Rose Bowl, had first met Autry as a youth in Oklahoma, where Reynolds' father was a driller in the oil fields, the same fields in which his son spent the summers. Reynolds ultimately went on to play professional football with the Detroit Lions, owned by George A. Richards, Autry's predecessor as owner of KMPC, where Reynolds, having been given a job by Richards, worked his way up from salesman to general manager. When Richards died and his family needed to sell KMPC to cover the estate taxes, Reynolds evidenced interest while also expressing need for a backer. Horace Lohnes, a partner in the law firm that represented both Autry and Reynolds, suggested the union.

KMPC was purchased for $800,000, with the lawyers creating the package in which Autry owned 56% of the station and Reynolds 30%, the other shares being made available to key employees. Reynolds became president of Golden West and Autry chairman of the board, the same positions they would assume with the Angels. They were friends and business partners, and when Autry said, "You know, Bob, I don't know why we shouldn't do it, why we shouldn't bid for the franchise ourselves, if only to protect the broadcast rights," Reynolds quickly agreed.

Autry's next step was to call Cronin at the American League office. He had known the league president since the days when Cronin was the shortstop and boy manager of the Washington Senators. Cronin was later managing the Boston Red Sox when Autry took the Gene Autry Rodeo into Boston Gardens. It was before a Saturday matinee there that Cronin knocked at the stage door, his three sons at his side.

"Think we could get in to see Gene?" he asked Pat Buttram.

"Sure," replied Buttram. "Don't know whether the boys will be more excited seeing Gene or he'll be more excited seeing you."

The Cronins visited with Autry while Buttram raced off to find three cowboy hats that Autry later autographed for the youngsters. That memory may have been with Cronin when Autry called.

"I hear Greenberg and Veeck have pulled out of the running for the team here," Autry said, getting right to the point. "I'd be interested in taking it, Joe. We have a group of radio stations out here. We used to carry the Dodger games. I once had stock in the Hollywood Stars team in the Pacific Coast League. I've been a baseball fan all my life. Would there be any objection if we applied?"

"None that I know of," Cronin said. "The question is one of time. There's another group. We'd need O'Malley's permission, your financial statement, information on what stadium you'd play in and a letter of credit. We'd need the letter by Monday."

It was Friday.

"How big a letter?" Autry asked.

"Million and a half," Cronin said.

The letter was there on time, and Autry soon followed it, traveling to a joint American and National League meeting that began December 5 at the Park Plaza Hotel in St. Louis. He was accompanied by Reynolds, by longtime baseball man Fred Haney (serving in an advisory capacity) and by Paul A. O'Bryan, a Washington, D.C., attorney who had met Autry through his role as counsel to the Federal Communications Commission and who would later become a stockholder in the Angels.

An agreement in which the American League would accept the National League's expansion into New York in 1962 paved the way for O'Malley's acceptance of an American League franchise in Los Angeles in 1961, and Cronin's memory of a long-ago favor paved the way for the American League's acceptance of Autry.

"Anybody who loves kids that much," Cronin told the owners, "has to be good for baseball."

Autry was approved on December 7, a date that will live in infamy and confirmation that the calendar had taken a curious turn. Exactly 19 years before, Donald Barnes, then owner of the financially and artistically beleaguered St. Louis Browns, had gone to the baseball meetings in St. Louis carrying documentation that he believed would justify his desire to move to Los Angeles. The meetings began December 8, 24 hours after the Japanese had bombed Pearl Harbor. There was speculation that California would be attacked next. Barnes' papers went into a trash can. The Gold Coast would remain untapped until 1958, discovered first by the National League.

O'Malley was among the first to congratulate Autry. The St. Louis meeting had no sooner ended than O'Malley extended an invitation to his suite. It was hardly a social affair. There, until three in the morning, over room-service dinner and repeated calls for coffee, the new owners received a proper introduction to the power and persuasiveness of the man who was frequently credited with being baseball's real commissioner. O'Malley's was the final word as they hammered out an arrangement in which the Los Angeles Angels of the American League would play the 1961 season in 20,500-seat Wrigley Field, former home of the Los Angeles Angels of the Pacific Coast League, and then move into the stadium O'Malley was building in Chavez Ravine. Autry agreed to a four-year lease with the option to renew for three.

When he emerged from the meeting, he confided to Reynolds and O'Bryan that he believed the club would be unhappy with some of the provisions, that joint tenancy wouldn't work, that he would never take advantage of the option. But this was a time of elation and exhilaration. He was thrilled to be in, to be part of that private society of club owners. The problems, if any, could wait. His euphoria was such that he could laugh along with those who noted that he had received help in assembling the needed capital from a four-legged associate named Champion.

"For the first time in baseball history," columnist Red Smith wrote, "a franchise has been awarded to an entire horse."

Autry agreed to pay $2.1 million for the 28 players he would select in the expansion draft and $350,000 indemnification to O'Malley for what Autry called "grazing rights" in Los Angeles. He had everything now except for a bat, ball, players and organization. The next morning, after four hours' sleep, he acquired his first player.

Autry and Haney had breakfast with second baseman Red Schoendienst and catcher Del Rice. Both had played for the Milwaukee Braves when Haney managed the Braves to National League pennants in 1957 and 1958. Both lived in St. Louis and both were now free agents, this being 15 years before that categorization was thought of in terms of multiyear contracts and millions of dollars. Rice and Schoendienst were simply out of work and of the opinion they could still play. Autry offered the opportunity to both. Schoendienst said he was committed to the Cardinals. Rice said that while he had never lived in Los Angeles, he would accept. The Angels had a 38-year-old catcher and Autry was on his way.

He was also on his way back to Los Angeles. It was December 8, just 24 hours after he had received the franchise, a little more than three months since O'Malley switched stations. Autry, Reynolds and Haney drove right from the airport to a press conference at the Sheraton Town House on Wilshire Boulevard. They walked into the lobby and Reynolds pulled Autry aside.

"Gene," he said, "we can't walk in there without a general manager. What about Fred? He's got the qualifications. Let's offer him the job."

Haney *had* a job. He was under contract to NBC as an analyst on their Game of the Week telecasts, after having served in just about every baseball capacity. He had been a scrappy, no-quarter-given-or-asked Detroit teammate of Ty Cobb. He had been a manager, general manager and broadcaster in the minors. He had been manager of a world championship team. Haney had done it all and seen it all. He was a resident of Los Angeles, respected and well liked throughout the game, and he was happy with NBC.

"It's going to be five to ten years before these people see daylight," Haney told wife Florence after accepting Autry's and Reynolds' offer to accompany them to St. Louis as advisor. "If anything were to come from this, the only thing I wouldn't mind doing is broadcasting their games."

Now, in the lobby of the Sheraton Town House, still under contract to NBC, Haney thought about the proposition just offered by Autry and Reynolds, thought about the immense job of building an organization from dust, of the five to ten years before daylight, and said, "Yes. If you have that kind of faith in me, I have that kind of belief in myself. It's a challenge, but we can do it."

It was only moments later that Haney was introduced to the media as the club's general manager, and only moments later that the former NBC analyst was asked if he had decided yet on his choice of managers. Haney said no, but in actuality the answer was yes. He had discussed the obvious choice with Autry and Reynolds on the flight from St. Louis. All three thought it was a natural. All three wanted Casey Stengel as their manager.

The irrepressible Stengel had managed the Yankees from 1949 through 1960. He won ten pennants, talked in a language few could understand and seemed totally out of place in a uniform, a bent and wrinkled man who had been unpopularly fired by the Yankees at age 70. Autry and Haney knew what kind of a team they would have, and they felt that Stengel's flair and wit would provide entertainment while the team struggled to attain respectability. Stengel was hot dogs, apple pie and Chevrolet. The Angels, competing in the shadow of the Dodgers, faced a struggle for survival—on and off the field.

Autry invited Stengel, who lived in suburban Glendale, to lunch at his Hollywood Hills home. They sat on the patio by the pool and talked for two hours, Stengel discoursing on everything from economy to ecology. Finally, growing impatient, Autry said, "Yes, Casey, but what about the job? Will you take it?"

Stengel shook his head. He told Autry that he would like to but that he had two problems. The first was that he had signed a lucrative contract to serialize his story in *The Saturday Evening Post,* and part of the agreement was that he had to stay out of baseball until the story had appeared. The second was that he had just become a director and stockholder of a Glendale bank, and he needed to spend some time there. Stengel said his situation would be different in a year, but knew the Angels couldn't wait even a week.

A year later, of course, Stengel was hired to manage the New York Mets. The marriage would become looked on as one made in Heaven, although the same might have been said if Stengel had accepted the Angels' offer, since there were times the Angels were every bit as "Amazin' " as the mediocre Mets.

Instead, however, with the expansion draft scheduled for Boston on December 14, the Angels quickly turned to their list of applicants and narrowed the choice to two: the controversial Leo Durocher and a Durocher disciple, Bill Rigney, who had succeeded Durocher as manager of the Giants in 1956 and had been fired in June of 1960 with his team in second place.

Durocher, a colorful umpire-baiter known as The Lip, a man who once said, "Nice guys finish last," represented some of the same qualities as Stengel, an instant opportunity to battle the Dodgers for the top half of the sports page. Yet Haney was concerned that Durocher would be unable to retain his patience with a team that figured to finish near the bottom in 1961 and for several summers after that.

"If we were going to have a winner right away, a really good club," Haney told Autry, "I wouldn't hesitate to hire Leo. But this is going to be the type of team that will test a manager's patience and temper. I'm not sure Leo can handle it. Rig's a fine manager and I think he'd be better suited for what we're going to go through."

A few weeks earlier, Rigney had been one of two finalists for the position as successor to Detroit manager Joe Gordon. The Tigers chose Bob Scheffing. Rigney, believing he had been unjustly fired in San Francisco, was keenly disappointed again. He restlessly spent the days playing golf and making phone calls, hoping to find a job. Then he heard Autry and Reynolds had been awarded the Los Angeles franchise. He quickly sent off a letter of application.

And he was soon en route to Los Angeles, flying in from his San Francisco area home to have dinner with the owners. The date: December 11. The next day Rigney became the first manager of the Angels, a position he would hold for more than eight years, with the next eight producing seven successors.

Rigney, believing that with an expansion team he required a measure of security, the assurance that he'd get more than a year to construct his building blocks, asked for and received a three-year contract.

The contract was an antacid of sorts, since the performance of the Angels would constantly eat at the ulcer of an animated man whose intensity was on a par with Durocher's and whose temper could occasionally match that of The Lion, another Durocher sobriquet.

This, however, was four months before the Angels would play their first game and about six months before a doctor would recommend to Rigney that he keep a piece of sponge cake and a glass of milk near the dugout as a midgame retardant for his flaming stomach. It was also about seven months before the cake and milk began to mysteriously disappear before Rigney could get to it. He ultimately discovered that catcher Earl Averill had been pilfering the snack. When finally apprehended, Averill said, "Hell, Rig, I thought it was there as a treat for the players."

This was December 12. Rigney huddled briefly with Haney and then flew home to pack for the trip to Boston. He was met at the San Francisco airport by his close friend, Giants general manager Charles (Chub) Feeney, who six months earlier had the unfortunate assignment of informing Rigney that owner Horace Stoneham had decided on a managerial change. This time Feeney did Rigney a favor. He handed him an envelope containing the Giants' scouting reports on the American League teams.

Rigney had spent his entire career in the National League, and now he had 48 hours to prepare for the selection of a team to compete in the American League. The Giants' reports were one source of information. Another was Casey Stengel, who briefed Haney, a National League veteran like Rigney, on the players Stengel suspected would be on the draft list, particularly the Yankees. The Angels also got a helping hand from an unexpected source. E. J. (Buzzie) Bavasi, then general manager of the Dodgers, agreed to provide close friend Haney with the Dodgers' American League reports. Bavasi might have refused, believing it was to the Dodgers' advantage to see the Angels stutter and stumble, leaving the Los Angeles market to O'Malley, but a long and warm relationship with Haney prompted him to respond favorably.

Walter O'Malley, sounding a bit facetious, told reporters, "We want them to be a happy tenant when they move into the new stadium in 1962."

Now Rigney and Haney had their paperwork for the flight to Boston, where the Angels and Senators would select 28 players at $75,000 each. Del Rice would soon have some teammates. Gene Autry would soon have a team for his franchise. Autry knew he would get the dregs, the players their current teams didn't want, but he couldn't have been more confident, more filled with anticipation.

Pat Buttram told him that the purchase of the club was the wisest move he had ever made. "Hell, Gene," he said, "on the sports pages a man can live forever. Look at Dempsey. They still call him 'Champ.' Look at DiMaggio. He's been retired for years and he's now bigger than ever. If he was an actor out of work he'd be looked on as a has-been. I mean it, Gene. On the sports pages you never die."

Chapter

III

AT THE press conference where it was announced that he had agreed to become general manager of the Angels, Fred Haney told the media that it felt strange to be in charge of a team that had everything except players and equipment. The next day Haney received a special delivery package from Chub Feeney of the Giants. In it was a bat, accompanied by a message that read, "Now you're on your way."

And now Haney and Bill Rigney were on their way to Boston to select the players who would swing the bat. They were armed with the Dodgers' and Giants' scouting reports and a differing philosophy as to which players they should select. Haney believed that the Angels had to make an immediate impact on the Los Angeles market, cutting into the Dodgers' popularity. He believed that the club had to acquire as many veteran or "name" players as possible, providing the Angels with instant identity.

Rigney understood that part of it, but also believed the An-

gels needed to build a base for the future, that since it would
be several years before the club's farm system was producing
major league players, they had to try to obtain the best of a
slim number of young players that the established eight teams
had exposed to the draft.

"Don't forget," Feeney had told him, "you're going to be
playing for many years, not just 1961."

The scouting reports provided the Angels with clues to the
ability of an otherwise anonymous group of young players,
clues the Washington Senators, represented in the draft meeting by manager Mickey Vernon and general manager Ed Do-
herty, lacked.

A year later, in fact, Senators owner Elwood (Pete) Quesada
invited Rigney to play golf on an off day in the capital and
asked, plaintively, "What led you to draft those kids? How
did you know about them?" Quesada referred to players such
as Bob Rodgers, who would be the Angels' catcher for almost
seven years; shortstop Jim Fregosi, a six-time All-Star and
future manager; and pitchers Fred Newman and Dean Chance,
the latter a future winner of the Cy Young Award.

While the Senators quickly strangled on the old age and
ineptitude of their expansion selections, the Angels' blend of
young and old helped maintain a modest respectability, but
the quality of players moving up from the farm system did not
give the Angels a winning team.

That failure, stemming from a network of scouts who, for
the most part, qualified for jobs only because of their friend-
ship with Haney and an alleged policy that discriminated
against the signing of blacks, ultimately destroyed the foundation Haney and Rigney constructed out of the meager offer-
ings in Boston, which Haney had enhanced with some early
trades.

The league's expansion plan called for the eight established
teams to submit a list of 15 players from their 40-man rosters.
A price of $75,000 was set for each player to be picked, and
each of the new clubs was required to select 28, at least 3 but
no more than 4 from each of the older clubs. Both the Angels
and Senators were required to pick 10 pitchers, 2 catchers, 6
infielders and 4 outfielders. There were no position restrictions
placed on the other 6 players.

Haney and Rigney flew to New York and took a train to Boston, a severe snowstorm having closed airports and delayed the draft by a day, giving the two California officials another 24 hours to study the reports. They were up until three that morning, conducting mock drafts, making sure that no matter how it went in a few hours, they would emerge with representation at each position, a player capable of opening the season, at least.

The draft was conducted in the American League office, with a coin flip determining who would select first for each position. The Angels saw it as a promising omen when Haney won three of the four flips, losing only when it came time to draft outfielders. He had already made the historic first selection in baseball's first-ever expansion draft, picking pitcher Eli Grba, a 26-year-old right-hander from the New York Yankees. The selection was based on the recommendation of Grba's former manager, Casey Stengel, under whom Grba won 6 of 10 decisions in 1960. Some four months later the Angels won their first-ever regular season game, beating Baltimore, 7–2, with Grba pitching a six-hitter and Stengel, the man the Angels wanted as their manager, getting an assist.

Grba, whose name seemed to be missing a vowel, provided headline writers with material such as "Grba Ptchs 4-Httr." He always said that being the first pick was a greater thrill than winning that first game. He was the first of 30 selections, Haney dipping into Autry's saddlebags for $2,150,000. Less than two decades later Autry would be giving that and more to individual players while saying, "I've already hocked the saddle. All I've got left is the horse."

The 30 included 2 players selected at $25,000 each from a minor league pool. They were first baseman Steve Bilko, one of the most popular athletes ever to perform in Los Angeles while playing first base for the minor league Angels and leading the Pacific Coast League in homers with 37, 55 and 56 in 1955–56–57; and outfielder Albie Pearson, the littlest Angel at 5-5 and 140 pounds. Pearson was selected from the Baltimore system while Bilko had been property of Detroit. The Angels benefited from both acquisitions, particularly that of Pearson, who shared Bilko's popularity. Pearson ultimately became the club's first .300 hitter and participated in one of Rigney's most interesting maneuvers.

The manager elected to room the diminutive Pearson with 6-2, 240-pound first baseman Ted Kluszewski, who promptly set down the rules. "I get the bed and you get the dresser drawer," Klu informed Pearson. A few months later, Klu came in late one night, lifted Albie out of bed, and attempted to prove to him that he would indeed fit in the drawer.

Kluszewski, a power hitter out of the Bilko mold, was one of those 30 players selected in the draft, his name submitted by the Chicago White Sox after he had concluded a distinguished career with the Cincinnati Reds. He was 37 at the time of the draft and, to some measure, characteristic of the type of player the Angels and Senators encountered on the big board in the American League office. They were players whose skills seemed eroded by time, or fringe players whose skills seemed of questionable nature. There was also that small group of young players exposed to the draft by clubs that hoped to sneak them through, clubs that believed the anonymous names would not be familiar to the drafting executives, particularly those with National League experience.

Rigney would later say that he had no illusions about the abilities of the organization's selections but that he was exhilarated to have at least emerged with a small nucleus for the future.

The Angels selected:

Pitchers: Dean Chance and Ron Moeller, Baltimore; Jerry Casale and Fred Newman, Boston; Ken McBride, Chicago; Aubrey Gatewood and Bob Sprout, Detroit; Bob Davis and Ned Garver, Kansas City; Truman Clevenger, Minnesota; Eli Grba and Duke Maas, New York.

Catchers: Ed Sadowski, Boston; Earl Averill, Chicago; Bob Wilson, Cleveland; Bob Rodgers, Detroit.

Infielders: Don Ross, Baltimore; Jim Fregosi, Boston; Ted Kluszewski, Chicago; Ken Aspromonte and Gene Leek, Cleveland; Eddie Yost, Detroit; Ken Hamlin, Kansas City; Julio Becquer, Minnesota; Steve Bilko, Denver (Detroit).

Outfielders: Jim McAnany, Chicago; Faye Throneberry, Minnesota; Bob Cerv and Ken Hunt, New York; Albie Pearson, Rochester (Baltimore).

Cynics looked at the list and predicted that the Angels wouldn't win 50 games. Autry looked at the list and asked colleague Buttram if he was positive that on the sports pages you never die.

Haney and Rigney knew they had work to do. They returned to Los Angeles, the city displaying great restraint in refraining from a premature parade, aware, perhaps, that the owner and his executives wouldn't have the time.

Autry was busy rounding up additional capital, attracting both Joseph Thomas, senior partner in Lehman Brothers, a New York stock firm, and J. D. Stetson Coleman, a wealthy investment associate of Thomas's. Both became minority stockholders and members of the board of directors. Tire magnate Leonard K. Firestone also joined the board, purchasing 30% of the stock after Reynolds and O'Bryan had traveled to his Palm Springs estate to discuss the new club.

Haney, having moved the organization into offices on Sunset Boulevard in downtown Los Angeles, about a tape-measure home run from Wrigley Field, was busy filling out his staff and deciding on a spring training site. The wisdom of his front office selections could be measured by ensuing developments and the fact that other organizations continually raided Haney's staff.

Marvin Milkes, a minor league executive when hired as assistant general manager, went on to become general manager of the Seattle Pilots and Milwaukee Brewers before assuming executive positions with other teams in various sports. Cedric Tallis, a minor league executive when hired as business manager, went on to become general manager of the Kansas City Royals and then vice president of the Yankees. Roland Hemond, farm director at Milwaukee when hired in the same capacity by Haney, went on to become vice president of the White Sox. Tom Ferguson, equipment manager at Milwaukee when hired as equipment manager by the Angels, became the club's traveling secretary and then a vice president at Milwaukee.

The hirings took several weeks. Haney was back from the draft meetings only a day when he closed the deal on a spring training base. It was December 16, less than nine days since Autry and Reynolds had been awarded the franchise. Now there were players and a place for them to train. Haney settled on Palm Springs, a desert resort some 120 miles from Los Angeles. It was a decision the club's players applauded for years.

A retreat for the rich and famous, Palm Springs offers a variety of plush golf courses, fine restaurants and neon hunting grounds. There is a pool in every backyard, a bar on every other corner, a bikini on every girl.

While all of the other spring camps were in Florida or Arizona, Haney announced he had selected Palm Springs because of his belief that a California team should train in California and because of its proximity to the Angels' new fans and Golden West Broadcasting's new sponsors.

Since then, at one time or another, every Angels manager has wondered just how much and what kind of training his players do in Palm Springs. Two-a-day workouts came to have a new meaning. Rigney shook his head once and muttered, "I'm not sure whether my players have a tougher time with fundamentals or the curfew."

The manager walked into the popular Howard Manor one night and prompted an evacuation that rivaled Dunkirk. Players were seen diving under tables and out windows.

The Angels initially stayed at the sprawling Desert Inn in the heart of the city. The writers lived in a home designed originally for actress Marion Davies near the front of the Inn. The scribes' lair, known as the Fourth Estate, became a 2 A.M. haven for bartenders, cocktail waitresses and musicians. There was a party every night. If Rigney had to find his players, he knew where to look. He often found them and fined them.

He also decided in the spring of 1963 that he was going to have the players ride bicycles to and from the workouts. He said if it didn't get them in shape, it might, at least, keep them so tired they would be reluctant to join the nightly chase. The plan worked only until the morning that the majority of bikes were found in the bottom of the hotel pool.

Eventually, while reluctant to sever all ties to Palm Springs, the Angels entered negotiations with the city of Holtville and opened a four-diamond training facility there in 1966. If Palm

Springs was bright lights, Holtville was no lights, the self-styled "Carrot Capital of the World," located 123 miles from Palm Springs in the agriculturally rich Imperial Valley.

The facility was built on a 21-acre sheep field and the Angels signed a 15-year lease, agreeing to a rent of $10,000 a year. The concept called for the Angels to spend the first 7 to 10 days of their spring camp there, taking advantage of the hot sun and Spartan environment to get their minds and bodies tuned to the game before facing the temptations of Palm Springs, after which the farm clubs would be chained and dragged to Holtville.

Then general manager Dick Walsh, angered at the Angels' poor play in 1973, ordered the 1974 club to Holtville for a full two weeks, saying, "After the disappointment of last year I felt it necessary to keep the club away from the bright lights as long as possible, to get it thinking only baseball."

Inevitably, however, there were so many complaints from both players and media regarding the absence of eating and recreational facilities in the Holtville area, so many occasions when the veteran players held out until the team got to Palm Springs, so many times when players were fined for missing curfew, having made the treacherous drive to Palm Springs, that the club decided to return to the spa on a full-time basis.

The farm teams still train in the farming heartland, but the varsity is back on the same diamond where Rigney issued his first call in 1961, back in the same stadium where a former president, Dwight D. Eisenhower, came to watch the exhibition games of that spring, back in the same clubhouse where second baseman Ken Aspromonte sat in March of 1961 and said, "We're going to fool a lot of people. We've been called rinky-dinks and fringe players. Well, that's wrong. A lot of us are guys who only need a break. We're a bunch of angry men."

Chapter

IV

THOSE ANGRY men would soon provide Autry with his greatest baseball thrill. But the first order of business at that first spring camp was a "Welcome Angels" banquet at the Desert Inn. Autry was asked to say a few words and responded by telling the audience that the club had made a strong attempt to secure Casey Stengel as the manager but had settled for a man the owners were sure would do a good job. He then introduced Bill Rigney as Phil Wrigley.

If Autry had made the same kind of faux pas when he first tried out for the Fields Brothers Marvelous Medicine Show he might never have gotten out of Tioga. Fortunately, perhaps, Autry was having so much trouble enunciating that few in the audience understood what he was trying to say. Then again the owner might be excused for his celebrative mood since this was the first time he had seen his team together.

At any rate, the humbling start didn't seem to affect Rigney, who was happy to be working, happy to have the opportunity,

Gene Autry, owner of the California Angels, on opening day.

In 1963 Jim Fregosi was a 21-year-old shortstop with a keen batting eye and a strong arm. He went on to an outstanding career with the Angels and became one of owner Gene Autry's "favorite sons." Appointed manager of the Angels in 1979, Fregosi was replaced by Gene Mauch in May, 1981. Picture A: Fregosi and an Angels coach. Picture B: Jim Fregosi, Angels manager, in the dugout as the Angels defeated the Yankees 2–1 on May 5, 1981.

In 1974 Angels manager Dick Williams (right) named Frank
Robinson captain of the Angels. Robinson, one of the game's great
home run sluggers (he hit 49 in 1966 with the Orioles), was traded by
the L.A. Dodgers to the Angels in 1973.

Sensational Nolan Ryan has just no-hit the Baltimore Orioles,
June 1, 1975, and poses with his catcher, Ellie Rodriguez, and Dick
Williams (right) his manager. It was Ryan's fourth no-hit game.

Bobby Grich, a free agent in 1976, signed a lucrative contract with owner Gene Autry of the Angels. One of the truly outstanding second basemen in baseball, Grich had several disappointing seasons, but in 1981 Bobby, then a 10-year major league star, had his finest season. He slugged 21 home runs and hit for a team-leading .302 average.

Don Baylor played out an option year with the Oakland team in 1976, then signed a six-year, $1.6 million contract with Angels owner Gene Autry. A solid, hard-hitting outfielder–first baseman, Baylor smashed 25 home runs in 1977 and then had his best year in baseball as he drove out 34 home runs in 1978.

Joe Rudi starred for three championship Oakland A's teams in 1973, 1974 and 1975, then played out his option year and signed with the Angels in 1977. An outfielder and outstanding first baseman, Rudi signed a five-year, $2 million contract with the Angels.

On June 18, 1979, Angel ace Nolan Ryan pitched seven innings of no-hit baseball before Texas Ranger Oscar Gamble singled to left and snapped Ryan's bid for his fifth no-hit game. The Angels defeated the Rangers 5–0 as Ryan gave up two hits. In 1979, after a magnificent nine-year career with the Angels, Ryan became a free agent and signed with the Astros.

Fred Lynn (left) and Angel coach Preston Gomez seem happy about the lucrative contract that brought Lynn into the Angels' camp. Lynn, one of the brightest outfield stars in recent Red Sox history, became a free agent and signed with the Angels prior to the 1981 season.

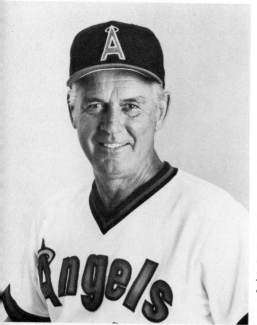

Gene Mauch took over as manager of the Angels in May, 1981, replacing Jim Fregosi. Previously the manager of the Minnesota Twins, the Phillies and the Expos, Mauch began his 22nd year as a major league manager. He was voted the National League Manager of the Year three times. Mauch started his professional baseball career as a shortstop in the Brooklyn Dodger farm system in 1943 and was singled out by Branch Rickey, who called him one of the smartest young baseball men he had ever met.

Butch Hobson, Angels third baseman, makes one of those "impossible" plays as he goes down on his knees for a line drive by ex-teammate Jim Rice as the Angels defeated the Red Sox in a game on June 11, 1981. Hobson was traded to the Angels with Rick Burleson on December 10, 1980; while Rick Miller, Carney Lansford and Mark Clear were sent to the Red Sox in one of the year's most important deals.

Before the 1980 season, pitcher Bruce Kison, a free agent, signed a five-year, $2.4 million contract with the Angels. Kison, a Pittsburgh Pirate from 1971 to 1978, doesn't appear happy in this photo. In the background, Harold Baines of the White Sox is circling the bases after a solo home run hit off Kison in a game on September 25, 1981.

Rick Burleson, a three-time All-Star, was acquired by the Angels, prior to the 1981 season. Burleson, a strong, aggressive shortstop, appeared in 106 games for the Angels and hit .295 for the season.

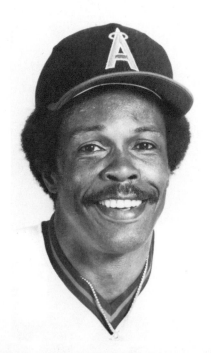

The 1981 season was a comparatively poor one for the Angels' Rod Carew, who hit .302 for the year. The seven-time American League batting champion sports a .334 batting average for his 15-year major league career and is a Hall-of-Fame certainty once he becomes eligible. Carew was signed to a five-year, $4 million contract in 1979 by Angels owner Gene Autry.

like his castoff players, to prove he could still do the job, anxious to show Horace Stoneham he had made a mistake.

Rigney had fired a needle in Stoneham's direction on his first day as Angels manager by saying, "Fred Haney has assured me that I'm in charge on the field, that he'll never second-guess me. I don't know if I can manage that way."

Rig quickly became a favorite of the Angels' press corps. He was glib and accessible, capable of providing stories when there were none, which was frequently the case with a team that would lose far more often than it would win, a team that was constantly putting a torch to Rigney's ulcer.

Example: Rigney's concentration during the critical moments of a game in Washington was shattered by a tapping on his shoulder. He turned to find catcher Earl Averill, who said, "I just counted, skipper, and there's eighty lights out in this stadium."

Example: Shortstop Fritz Brickell fielded a double-play grounder and threw it into right field, where Albie Pearson retrieved it and threw it wildly to the middle of the infield, where pitcher Ron Kline retrieved it and threw it wildly to third base. There had been three errors on the same play and now the ball was bouncing toward the dugout, where Rigney fielded it, stared at it ("I thought about taking a bite out of it") and finally put it in a secure place, his hip pocket.

Example: The Mets had Marvelous Marv Throneberry. The Angels had his brother, Fabulous Faye. In the late innings of a tense game, Rigney called on Faye to pinch-hit. He called and called. Faye was asleep in the corner of the dugout.

Example: The Angels held a slim lead in the late innings of a game at Minnesota. The Twins had loaded the bases against Dean Chance, who delivered a pitch low and away. Catcher Hank Foiles reached for it, then spun and raced to the backstop screen, where he searched in vain for the ball. All three runners scored before Foiles thought to look in his glove. The ball had been there all the time.

"The lunatics," Rigney once observed, "have taken over the asylum."

The takeover had actually begun when 275 "athletes" of all descriptions showed up at a Los Angeles tryout camp in early

February, 1961. Six were signed to professional contracts. One, pitcher Morris Cigar, performed impressively in spring training before being sent to the minors, where his brief career expired. His Palm Springs roommate was another product of that tryout camp and the first player cut in that first Palm Springs camp. He was a penniless, dispirited infielder whom equipment manager Tom Ferguson sent off with a tuna sandwich. His name was Charlie Pride and he would soon find better days in another area of the entertainment business.

Pride and Cigar, two names that offered intriguing possibilities to the hungry journalists, were gone before Haney began shaping a team that boasted power and little else. The general manager knew he would have to deal and he did. The Angels made 21 transactions involving 30 players in 1961 and 20 involving 24 in 1962. Ryne Duren, Lee Thomas, Joe Koppe, Billy Moran, Art Fowler, Tom Morgan, Leon Wagner—those and other names so important to the Angels during the first few summers were acquired either through trade, purchase or free agent signing.

Marvin Milkes, Haney's new aide, had broad minor league experience and knew where to look and with whom to talk. This was also baseball's first expansion. There were only 18 teams. The talent wasn't as diluted as it has become with 26 teams. There were players performing at the triple A level who were capable of doing a job in the majors.

Joe Koppe and Billy Moran, for instance, were both acquired in minor league maneuvers. They replaced Ken Hamlin and Ken Aspromonte as the Angels' shortstop and second baseman in midseason and provided strength up the middle during a surprisingly successful 45-44 second half.

Leon Wagner, who led the Angels in home runs with 28 in 1961, 37 in 1962 (a club record for 16 years) and 26 in 1963, was obtained during the season's first week when Feeney reminded Rigney of the ex-Giant outfielder's potential, and Rigney reminded Haney, who authorized Milkes to open negotiations with Jack Kent Cooke, owner then of the minor league team in Toronto, where Wagner was playing.

The new Angel contributed significantly to his team's attack and spirit. He delivered as many punch lines as line drives. He also led the club in requests for front office loans. The biggest was applied to a clothing store he opened on Crenshaw Boulevard in Los Angeles. The slogan "Get Your Rags From Daddy Wags" was of better quality than the merchandise and the creditors soon foreclosed. Wags told the Angels to deduct the debt from his paychecks. All of the favors seemed forgotten when Wagner was traded in a contract dispute after the 1963 season and called Haney a Khrushchev. Haney responded by calling a unique press conference at which he disclosed the history of the club's financial dealings with Wagner. Wagner quickly issued an embarrassed apology for having compared Haney to the then Russian premier, explaining it was only natural for anyone traded to Cleveland to have trouble thinking straight.

The biggest trade of the first season was consummated on May 9 when Haney sent pitcher Truman Clevenger and outfielder Bob Cerv to New York for relief pitcher Ryne Duren, first baseman–outfielder Lee Thomas and pitcher Johnny James, the ill-fated right-hander who would soon give new dimension to the term breaking ball, breaking his arm while throwing one.

Thomas hit 24 homers, drove in 70 runs and batted .285 while earning the nickname "Mad Dog" because of his temper. Thomas was playing golf with a sportswriter one day in 1961 when he became angered over a poor shot and hurled his driver with such force it tore through a chain-link fence. Thomas was soon joined by another Thomas, outfielder George, acquired from Detroit, and they formed a power package that came to be called T 'N T. Unfortunately, George's career ended early. He had trouble throwing. Twice in one season he lost his grip and threw the ball behind him.

Duren, nicknamed "The Flame" because of his sizzling fast-ball, became a valuable addition to a bullpen rebuilt entirely that first year, a bullpen that was the backbone of the team's modest success. It included Tom (The Plowboy) Morgan, left-hander Jack Spring (one of the few Angels without a nickname) and John Arthur Fowler, known as "King Arthur" and "The Hummer" because of his own lively fast-ball. Fowler was a 39-year-old right-hander acquired from the Dodgers' organization. He had helped pitch the Dodgers to the National League pennant in 1959 and was unceremoniously honored by being sent to the minors. Fowler had a simple philosophy: throw strikes and put a little something on it. The theory kept him in the majors at an age when most pitchers are in the unemployment line. Fowler was extraordinary with the Angels until the freak accident of 1962, in which he lost the sight in his left eye, diluted his effectiveness and perhaps deprived the Angels of a pennant in only their second year.

No story better characterizes the aplomb with which Fowler went about his job than this one: Pitcher Paul Foytack, having recently been acquired by the Angels, walked the bases loaded in the first inning of his first start. Fowler was summoned. Foytack handed him the ball and said, "I've been reading how good you are. Let's see you get out of this one." Fowler promptly struck out the side.

Duren also contributed his own chapter to the team's folk-lore. He was a free-spirited right-hander who wore thick glasses, always threw his first warm-up pitch against the back-stop screen in an effort to intimidate the hitter and had the tendency to become obstreperous when drinking, which was frequently. Now a rehabilitated alcoholic who heads alcohol abuse programs in Milwaukee, Duren once—

—Crashed into the hotel room of sportswriter Dan Hafner, flipping over both Hafner and the mattress he was sleeping on.

—Provided a 5:30 A.M. wake-up call for pitching coach Marv Grissom by chipping golf balls off his hotel room win-dow, prompting Grissom, accustomed to Duren's eccentrici-ties, to open the door and say, "Got kind of an early starting time, don't you Ryne?"

—Celebrated a 1–0 win in a rare starting assignment by wading through the ponds of a hotel's Polynesian restaurant in Cleveland. The restaurant manager called Rigney and said, "Mr. Rigney, I've got one of your players . . ."

"Don't tell me. I know exactly which one," Rigney inter-rupted. "I'll be right down."

The drunk Duren was always in a fight, suffering more knockouts than the bums Joe Louis confronted on a monthly basis. But he never remembered the next morning, never held a grudge and always gave 200%, a characteristic of the Angels during the early years.

The first official step for the "rinky-dinks" and "fringe players" was April 11 against Baltimore, on a cold, gray afternoon, with Eli Grba vs. Milt Pappas, the ace of a team favored to win the American League pennant.

At a party the night before the game, Autry sat next to a longtime friend, Baltimore manager Paul Richards. Richards put his arm around Autry's shoulders and said, "Well, cowboy, you're my pal, but tomorrow the bell rings and I'm going to have to beat your ass."

Autry raised his glass and said, "More power to you, Paul. I imagine you will."

Rigney started a lineup of Eddie Yost at third base, Ken Aspromonte at second, Albie Pearson in right field, Ted Kluszewski at first, Bob Cerv in left, Ken Hunt in center, Fritz Brickell at short. On the mound was Eli Grba, his catcher was Del Rice.

Autry and Reynolds had no sooner reached their seats and buttoned up their overcoats than the Angels exploded in the manner of their owner's six-shooter. Pearson walked and Klu homered to right. Cerv followed with a homer to center and it was 3–0 after the first inning with more to come. Pearson lined an RBI single in the second and Klu followed with another homer. It was 7–0 after two, and Grba's cushion was quite comfortable.

The final score was 7–2. The Angels led the American League with an undefeated record, and it was as if they had just won the seventh game of the World Series. They yelled and slapped each other on the back, making sport of things that had been said about them, of the predictions they wouldn't win 50 games.

Publicity director Irv Kaze invited Grba and the writers to his hotel room for champagne, and Grba said that while it wasn't really as big a thrill as being drafted No. 1, he would never forget the emotions he experienced when he handed the ball with which he had gotten the final out to Autry in the clubhouse.

Years later, in another clubhouse in another place, with the champagne flowing and his players celebrating the first title in the club's history, Autry would say that the victory on April 11 of 1961 was still his biggest thrill, his greatest moment.

Unfortunately, it was not long before the freshman Angels confronted the anticipated and predicted reality. They returned from that first trip with a 1-7 record, having lost 7 in a row after the opening victory while also being rained out 8 times. The rain-outs were rescheduled as part of a midsummer trip, creating a death march of 26 games in 20 days, the Angels winning only 7.

It was never routine.

Duren tied a major league record by striking out 4 batters in one inning, but only after Averill's failure to hold the spitball on the third strikeout led to the run that defeated the Angels.

Lee Thomas went 9-for-11 with 3 home runs and 8 RBIs in a doubleheader at Kansas City and the Angels lost both games.

Tied with the Yankees at 3–3 in the sixth inning of a game in which Duren set a club strikeout record with 12, Rigney, for reasons even the manager couldn't later explain, allowed Duren to bat with two runners in scoring position. Duren responded with a single, driving in the two decisive runs with only his third career hit.

The Angels lost 91 games that first year. They also won 70, a total that no expansion team has ever exceeded in its first year. The 50th win prompted a celebration that rivaled that of opening day. Ted Bowsfield pitched No. 50 and two weeks later reached a career high with win No. 10, prompting a personal celebration which included a unique reversal of roles. Two writers had to help the wobbly Bowsfield back to the team's hotel.

The Angels finished eighth, 38½ games behind the pennant-winning Yankees. But in the year that Roger Maris hit 61 homers and Mickey Mantle 54, the two New York sluggers hit a total of only 4 at cozy Wrigley Field, where the Angels and their opponents combined for 248, a major league record. Appropriately, the 248th came in the ninth inning of the season's 162nd and last game and was delivered in a pinch-hit role by Steve Bilko, the man who had authored those renowned minor league seasons in Wrigley.

The homer was Bilko's 29th, giving the Angels five players with 20 or more, the others being Wagner (28), Hunt (25), Thomas (24) and Averill (20). Hunt, buried behind Mantle in the Yankee system prior to the expansion draft, led the club in RBIs with 84, while Pearson was No. 1 in average at .288. Rigney got 12 wins from Ken McBride, 11 each from Grba and Bowsfield and some strong relief from Tom Morgan (8-2, 2.35 ERA) and Art Fowler (5-8, 3.64 ERA). Duren moved successfully and repeatedly between the bullpen and rotation, setting a league record, in addition to his other accomplishments, by striking out the first 7 hitters in a June 9 start at Boston.

The final month of the first season saw the recall of Jim Fregosi, Bob Rodgers, Dean Chance and Fred Newman, all of whom represented the promise of better days.

The Angels would move to Dodger Stadium in 1962, having drawn 603,510 for that first and last year at Wrigley Field, since torn down to make room for a housing project. The Dodgers, playing their fourth and last season at the nearby Coliseum while waiting for the 1962 opening of Dodger Stadium, drew 1.8 million. The Angels escaped the Dodgers' shadow only when Mantle, Maris and the Yankees came to town. The nine games with New York attracted 166,522 to the 20,500-seat stadium, twice as many as came to see any of the other visiting clubs.

The Angels attendance was a league low. Yet it was high enough, considering the club's small player payroll, low rent and absence of a farm system, to provide a sizable profit. However, the owners reacted in a curious fashion. Instead of allowing the profit to draw interest, to grow, to be used in the signing of prospects and the development of a farm system, Autry and associates decided to recoup their initial investment.

Ultimately, the bottom line on 1961 was a deceiving loss of almost $1 million, of which Robert Reynolds, years later, said, "It was a mistake, not putting the profit to use. If the decision had been strictly up to Gene and me, we might have decided differently. But we had promised the other investors that they would get their money back as soon as possible and we felt committed to honor that promise."

There would be other curious decisions carrying significant

ramifications, decisions that would begin to take their toll in the mid-1960s, strangling the growth of a promising franchise and extinguishing the glow that became even brighter in 1962, which would be remembered for reasons other than the owners' decision of the preceding winter. The 1962 season would be remembered for the arrival of Robert (Bo) Belinsky.

Chapter

V

NO ANGEL—no major league player ever—received more publicity for accomplishing less. He won the grand total of 28 games during a major league career that spanned six seasons. His highest salary was $18,000.

Five of those wins came in succession at the start of the 1962 season and included a May 5 no-hitter against Baltimore. Years later, he would say:

"The night before my no-hitter I met this tall, thin, black-haired secretary out at a place on the Sunset Strip. We had a couple drinks and I wound up making it with her at her pad. She wasn't bad. I got home about four A.M. and that night pitched my no-hitter. I went back to look for her after the game and couldn't find her. I never found her again. She was my good-luck pitching charm and, when I lost her, I lost all my pitching luck."

Nothing says more about the way Bo Belinsky went about it, about his philosophy, than that. He also used to say, "If you want a helping hand, look at the end of your own arm."

Bo's hand was most often wrapped around a waist or a glass. He briefly had it all, king of the hill in a manner he dreamed about while growing up on the streets and in the pool halls of Trenton.

He was 5-0 with a no-hitter, having made a mark even before his first win of that first big-league season, by staging a contract holdout that ended with a poolside press conference at the Desert Inn. It was an auspicious introduction and it only got better.

By mid-May Bo was the pal of syndicated columnist Walter Winchell and the hottest stud in Hollywood. He dated Ann-Margret, Tina Louise, Queen Soraya, Doris Duke, Paulette Goddard and a Du Pont heiress, among others. He eventually became engaged and disengaged to Mamie Van Doren. There was a party every night, Bo thinking it would never end, his religion being that of night walkers everywhere.

Teammate Dean Chance was his closest friend. A strange alliance: Belinsky, the street-smart left-hander from the big city of the East; Chance, the hayseed right-hander from the farm in Wooster, Ohio. Both were out of the Baltimore organization where they had barely known each other, only of each other. They soon became inseparable, one's problems becoming the other's, in a way that it was difficult to determine whether Bo was having the most damaging effect on Dean or Dean was having the most damaging effect on Bo.

Each had major league ability. Belinsky's forte was his screwball, and it was frequently written that nothing was more appropriate. Chance had as much talent as any pitcher of his time. His fast ball, dispensed from an intimidating full pivot during which Chance did not even look at the plate, featured both velocity and movement. Yet he had it together really for only two full seasons.

Nothing seemed to get through. Autry, Haney and Rigney took turns lecturing Bo and Dean. They were fined repeatedly. Bo was farmed out once (to Hawaii of all places). Ultimately, both were traded, the catalyst in Belinsky's expulsion being an incident in which he allegedly used a can of shaving cream to slug veteran sportswriter Braven Dyer, a man almost three times his age.

Bo was traded to Philadelphia for pitcher Rudy May and outfielder Costen Shockley in the winter of 1964, his three-year record with the Angels 20-28. The 5-0 start of 1962 ultimately turned to 10-11, followed by a 2-9 in 1963, the year he was sent to Hawaii, and a 9-8 in 1964, when his earned run average was a very good 2.87.

Chance, a prize plum from the expansion draft and yet a pitcher whom Bob Rodgers described as the "dumbest I ever caught," was traded to Minnesota in the winter of 1966 for first baseman Don Mincher, outfielder Jimmie Hall and pitcher Pete Cimino.

Chance won 74 games in his five seasons with the Angels, a victim frequently of ineffective and inconsistent support, a pitcher whose ability could be measured by his 22-4 record at Dodger Stadium during the 1964 and 1965 seasons when he was 7-0 against the dreaded Yankees.

In 1962, when Bo got off 5-0 and the Angels went on to stun the baseball world by finishing third, the 21-year-old Chance was 14-10, the winningest rookie in the American League. He was 13-18 with a 3.19 ERA in 1963, and he then became the youngest pitcher ever to win the Cy Young Award, turning in a 20-9 record with baseball's lowest ERA (1.65) in 1964, a year in which he pitched 14 games of five hits or less and manager Rigney called him "the best right-hander I've ever seen."

Chance may have enjoyed the same kind of year in 1965 except for what was described as an "abcessed tooth" but was believed to be an infection centered somewhat lower in his body. He appeared in about 15 fewer games than normal, winning 15 of 25 decisions with another good ERA, 3.15.

Chance's ERA (3.08) was again more reflective of his performances than a 12-17 record in 1966, after which the anemic Angels decided to trade him while his value was still high.

Five years after they had made their major league debuts— the Angels seeing in Belinsky a personality to counter the Dodgers' popularity and in Chance a talent around which to build their future—both were gone, only the memories lingering to be laughed at amid the frustration of what might have been. Even now, those memories—who they were, where they came from, what they did—seem fresh, the yesterdays melting away to reveal a tall, thin, good-looking Belinsky surrounded by reporters as he lounged next to the Desert Inn pool on a bright, warm March afternoon in 1962.

He was 25 then, the son of a Polish Catholic father and Russian Jew mother. What he learned, he said, he had learned on the streets. He was 10 when he had his first cigarette in the bathroom of a theater; 12 when he had his first relations with a girl, in the elevator of his grandmother's apartment. Hustlers named The Goose, The Farmer, Cincinnati Phil and The Lemonade Man broadened his education, introducing him to the three-cushion bank shot and life on the road.

Baseball then was a diversion, a Sunday sandlot game, a few dollars when the pockets were otherwise empty. The only name he really knew was that of Hal Newhouser, and only because Newhouser was also a lefty. Pittsburgh scout Rex Bowen saw one of those games and offered Bo $185 a month and a bus ticket to Brunswick, Georgia, site of the Pirates' Class A affiliate.

"What the hell," thought Bo, "what else am I doing? I mean, I think I was working in an overalls factory then, playing pool and fooling with the broads."

That was the start of it. Brunswick, Georgia, 1956. A long way from the Sunset Strip.

His route took him to Pensacola, Knoxville, Aberdeen, Amarillo, Stockton, Vancouver and Little Rock. He had modest success, winning 13 one year, 10 another, 9 another, his potential reflected by strikeout totals such as 202 in 195 innings, 183 in 174. His reputation grew in many ways. An 18-year-old Knoxville girl with whom he'd spent a night charged him with rape, and he was smuggled out of town on the floor of a friend's car. He and teammate Steve Dalkowski drilled holes in the wall of a Miami hotel room so they could watch one of the contestants in the 1961 Miss Universe contest, drawing the wrath of the hotel and their manager after Dalkowski shined a flashlight through one of the holes and the young lady became aware she was being watched. There was a fight in a Little Rock bar, and Belinsky was accused of having started it.

Bo moved from the Pittsburgh organization to the Baltimore organization. He didn't see much future and considered quitting. Harry Dalton, later a general manager of the Angels but then farm director of the Orioles, talked him out of it. It was the winter of 1961 and Bo was eligible for the annual draft, having been unprotected by the Orioles, who were rich in pitching talent and skeptical of Bo's behavior.

Fred Haney and scout Tuffie Hashem discussed possible selections, Hashem telling Haney that the one name that kept popping up in his conversations with minor league managers and coaches was that of Belinsky. Hashem said he had seen Bo pitch twice and felt he was a real prospect.

"Why hasn't anybody picked him up before?" Haney asked. "Got a bad arm?"

"No," Hashem said. "He's a wiry guy who can pitch regularly."

"What else is there about him?" Haney asked.

"Well," Hashem said, "you keep hearing the same things. Mention Belinsky's name and people smile at you like you're nuts. They say, 'Sure, we know Bo. He's got a million-dollar arm and ten-cent head.' "

Haney decided to find out for himself. He went to the winter meetings in Tampa armed with his top 20 draft choices. He first selected infielder Marlan Coughtry from Seattle. Coughtry played 11 games for the Angels, batting .182 before he was traded. Haney next selected infielder Felix Torres from Buffalo of the International League. Torres would play third for the Angels for three seasons, a kind man whose legs always appeared to be taking a siesta.

Finally, after the 20 clubs had selected 62 other minor leaguers, the Angels chose Belinsky, then pitching in the Venezuelan Winter League and unaware of his selection. He did not learn about it, in fact, until after he had returned to his Trenton home and opened the contract that called for a major league minimum of $6,000.

"I thought it was a joke," Bo said later, having told Haney the same thing over the phone. "I had played all those years in the minors and they were offering me the minimum like I was a kid with no record. I wouldn't sign. I told Haney that if he didn't give me $8,500 then I'd forget about baseball. The hell with it. I had a few things going in Trenton."

The Angels opened camp on February 24. The rookie left-hander wasn't there. Bud Furillo of the *Herald Examiner* called him.

"I'm not coming in for a penny less than $8,500," Bo told him.

"What are you doing to pass the time?" Furillo asked.

"Playing pool and laying a lot of broads," Belinsky replied.

Furillo said thank you and broke the land speed record getting to his typewriter. The *Herald* bannered the story of the pitcher who worshipped wine, woman and song, and suddenly Bo was a story from coast to coast.

"He was the greatest thing to ever happen to us," publicity director Irv Kaze conceded years later. "He put the Angels on the map. But I don't think he ever really cared about pitching and winning. He never seemed to care about anything. He had a terrific arm and could have been a star, but he wasn't motivated. I truly think he didn't give a damn if he played in the majors or minors."

Bo's holdout angered Haney, but he sensed the magic, the publicity value in getting Bo to camp. He called and said, "Look, why don't you come out and we'll negotiate here. You can talk to our owners. Maybe they'll give you some more money."

The idea appealed to Bo and he flew west.

"I'm Kaze, welcome to California," the publicity director said, meeting him at the airport.

"Christ," said Bo, "I thought you were Autry."

Kaze took Belinsky directly to a poolside press conference.

"It was like a movie," Bo said later. "They sat me down, poured me a drink and took off. They wanted names and dates of all the broads I had ever been with. They wanted to know about my pool playing and the fights I had been in. I gave them the answers they wanted to hear. Then they asked about the contract and I told them I wouldn't sign unless Autry begged me personally."

Three days passed and Haney finally summoned Bo to his room, saying it couldn't go on, that Bo had to sign or go home. Bo decided that he had begun to like the town and the team, and he agreed to sign providing the Angels would renegotiate his contract in midseason.

"If you make the club we'll take a look at it in midseason," Haney said. "I won't promise anything, but if you don't sign you're gone."

He was almost gone anyway.

The Angels decided a few weeks later that it didn't appear Bo had major league ability and that under those circumstances he wouldn't be worth the aggravation. They offered him back to the Orioles for $12,500, half of the draft price. The Orioles thanked the Angels for their generosity but said they weren't interested.

Belinsky reflected years later and said that while he always considered Haney a good guy, a class guy, he believed that Rigney was always "jealous of all the attention I got" and determined to prove "he was bigger than anyone on the team. He could manage the hell out of a game but he was strictly Joe Hollywood, wearing those dark shades and trying to let everyone know just how big a man he was around town."

Rigney wanted to send Belinsky to the minors, but pitching coach Marv Grissom urged that they take a longer look. The Angels headed for the season opener in Chicago with two rookie pitchers, Dean Chance and Bo Belinsky, on the 28-man squad that would be cut to 25 a month later.

It was two weeks later before Bo started for the first time, Rigney being devoid of alternatives for the April 19 day game against Kansas City at Dodger Stadium. Bo prepared in his customary fashion, getting to bed at four or five in the morning.

"Sex always relaxed me," he said. "Nobody ever died from it."

This time, however, Belinsky knew the importance of the next day's assignment. "I knew it was win or else," he said. "I knew I was just hanging on and that I would have been long gone if the writers hadn't made me a celebrity and the front office hadn't pressured Rigney into keeping me."

Bo responded by restricting Kansas City to two runs through seven innings. Art Fowler then came on to save what represented Belinsky's first major league victory. Four days later he beat Cleveland for No. 2, and five days later he went nine innings for the first time, shutting out Washington, 3–0.

Within ten more days he would have two more wins, including the no-hitter, which was that much sweeter since it came against the Orioles.

"Everybody wanted me at Hollywood parties," Belinsky said. "Playing baseball seemed only incidental. It was a little too much, even for me. I mean after hustling in pool halls and living on candy bars, this was something else."

This was never going to bed before 4 A.M., never going to bed alone. It was Walter Winchell and Ann-Margret and Tina Louise and Juliet Prowse. It was the promised raise to $8,500 and a candy-apple-red Cadillac convertible.

Suddenly the record that reached 6-1 began to deteriorate. Bo lost six of his next seven decisions. The girls didn't seem to mind, but the Angels did. They warned him about his night life and fined him for missing curfew. Rigney assigned pitching coach Grissom to room with him on the road. Bo never had to look hard for roomies at home.

One night, accompanied by Chance and two girls as he drove home from the customary party, Belinsky lost his cool. It was one of those times when Bo wasn't in the mood to hear his date tell him how much she loved him and wanted to stay with him. He pulled the car over and attempted to pull her out. The girl grabbed the door handle and held on, ultimately suffering facial cuts when her head crashed against the windshield. The melee and its accompanying screams attracted the police, and all four were taken to the nearest precinct, where the police attempted to get the girl to sign a complaint against Belinsky. She considered and then told Bo, "I won't sign if you promise to stay with me all week."

Belinsky, understanding the difference between discretion and valor, jumped at the proposition.

Years later, however, he said, "You think she showed any gratitude? Hell, no. She eventually got an attorney and sued me for $150,000. My lawyer had to give her a few bucks to get her out of town, to keep her mouth shut."

The incident created more headlines and the Angels responded by fining Belinsky and Chance, who was married at the time, $500 each. It was a particularly costly evening, but not one that changed the lifestyles of either Chance or Belinsky.

"Nobody," said Chance, looking back on their careers, "made it with girls the way Bo did. I never learned his secret, but I enjoyed trying."

Albie Pearson roomed with Bo briefly and said he had two jobs, one as a ballplayer and one as Bo's answering service.

"When I roomed with him," Pearson said, "it was like rooming with his suitcase. I'd never see him at night.

"One time we were on an eastern trip and got back to Los Angeles at three in the morning. We were really dragging. But we got off the plane and there's Winchell with three of the best-looking girls you've ever seen. Bo doesn't even wait for his bags. He takes off with Walter and the girls as the rest of the team watched and cheered. We knew Bo would have some good stories for us the next day."

Late in the 1962 season, with the Angels making their surprising pennant bid, Haney negotiated the acquisition of relief pitcher Dan Osinski from Kansas City for cash and a player to be named later, specifically Belinsky.

Trades of that type are made all the time, with the two clubs inevitably agreeing at the time of consummation on who the player to be announced later will be. In this instance, the Angels saw the need for another relief pitcher during the final weeks of the season. They'd also had enough of Bo's extracurricular activities, but were unable to trade him at that time because of waiver restrictions and because they didn't want to part with his arm during those final weeks.

Bo learned about his involvement in the trade from Kansas City manager Hank Bauer. He had no desire to give up Hollywood for a quiet little city in the Midwest, and he knew by making public the fact that the As and Angels had already agreed on his inclusion in the deal, and the fact that the Angels had already agreed to trade a player who might be pitching for them in the World Series, he would force the league office to investigate a procedure that goes on all the time.

Thus, after a game in New York, knowing he would get broadest coverage in the media capital, Belinsky announced, "I've been traded to the As as the player to be named later in the Osinski deal and I'm not going."

Both Haney and Rigney were livid. They knew at once that they could not now trade Belinsky and that they would spend the day making false denials. Commissioner Ford Frick said it was strictly an American League matter, and the American League said it was strictly a club matter. The buck finally stopped at the desks of Haney and the Kansas City owner, Charles Finley. They agreed Belinsky was no longer the player to be announced later; it would be pitcher Ted Bowsfield instead.

Belinsky could keep his Hollywood pad. He was still with the Angels, still rooming with Chance when they celebrated the end of the 1963 Palm Springs encampment with a little party that resulted in their reporting more than an hour late to the final workout. They had started the new season in the same manner they had closed the old one, drawing $500 fines each.

That was the good news. Some two months later, on May 26, Bo got the bad. He was summoned to Rigney's office and told that because of his 1-7 record he was being sent to Hawaii. Some bad news! It was love at first sight.

"I had a chance to pull myself together," he said. "Hollywood had been great, but in Hawaii I could set my own pace. I had also never seen so many beautiful girls in my life. The whole thing was out of this world."

So was Bo's pitching. He was 4-1 with a 2.50 ERA when recalled by the Angels in late August. Belinsky was depressed. He considered not reporting. Then he decided that the Angels still represented the brightest lights and flew back to a royal reception from the Hollywood crowd. He was 1-2 over the remainder of the season and was invited to do two weeks with comedian Hank Henry at the Silver Slipper in Las Vegas, receiving $1,000 a week. Chance flew in to visit him, blew $1,500 the first night and immediately flew home.

Belinsky returned to Hollywood for the rest of the winter and signed a 1964 contract for $15,500, a raise of $2,000 despite his horrendous season. He could also take comfort in a still warm relationship with Mamie Van Doren, would-be successor to Marilyn Monroe as Hollywood's sex symbol.

Bo and Mamie had met in 1962, introduced by her former husband, bandleader Ray Anthony. They were soon seen everywhere together, including the ball park, where Mamie became a fixture, bringing the Angels the type of publicity that they couldn't attain with their play.

"She's great to be with," Bo told the press, saying her only fault was that she didn't allow him to smoke in the bedroom.

The publicity and constant presence of the actress ultimately prompted Rigney to tell Bo that if he wouldn't spend so much time with Mamie, he might win more games. Bo bit his tongue. He wanted to tell his manager that if he also had more runs and better defense he might win more games.

The relationship with Mamie shifted between hot and cold, on and off, until finally, in April of 1963, in an effort, Belinsky would say later, to get the press off their back, Bo told reporter Bud Furillo that they were engaged. Furillo asked Mamie about it and she said, "If Bo says we're engaged, then we're engaged."

Engaging as it appeared, it didn't last. Bo wasn't ready to settle down, to confine himself to one woman.

"All of a sudden," he said, "Mamie became very possessive. She began to talk about a wedding date. I didn't know what she meant. Engaged is one thing. Married is a different game."

Bo wasn't ready to play and the engagement ultimately dissolved, Mamie returning his $2,000 diamond ring only after he had hired a detective to gather evidence that she was being as disloyal as she claimed Bo was.

Remarkably, the end of the engagement created new ardor, and Bo and Mamie remained good friends until she finally was successful in getting a left-handed pitcher to the altar, marrying 19-year-old Lee Meyers of the Chicago Cubs, who was killed several years later in a car accident.

Bo now speaks of Mamie in only the best of terms, and they were still good friends in 1964, his last year with the Angels, a year in which he again was twice fined $500. The first fine was levied during spring training when the team's Palm Springs hotel complained about the mess Bo and his female gymnastics partner had created when they failed to clean up a room service cart they had kicked over at the high point of their exercises. The second was levied when Bo stepped out of a cab in suit and tie at 4 A.M. and confronted Rigney and his teammates in their pajamas, having been routed by a fire at their Boston hotel.

The incident, however, that finally ended Bo's career with the Angels took place in the early hours of August 14, 1964, after Bo had been hit hard and victimized by poor defense in a loss to Cleveland at Dodger Stadium the preceding afternoon. Only Charles Maher, then of the Associated Press and now of the *Los Angeles Times,* went to the clubhouse to talk to Bo after the game. Belinsky was frustrated and discouraged and expressed those sentiments while also saying he was thinking about quitting. Maher reported it all in the context that Bo probably didn't mean it, since he was depressed after a tough defeat.

Maher wrote his story as the Angels and their press corps flew east for a series in Washington, D.C. The team arrived at the Shoreham Hotel about 1:30 A.M. Chance and Belinsky went out to dinner, returning about 3:00. They were in the room only a few minutes when the phone rang. It was Braven Dyer of the *Times.*

"I want to talk to you about that story you gave Maher about quitting," Dyer said, according to Bo.

"I didn't tell him I was quitting," Belinsky responded, "and who are you to tell me what I can and can't tell him?"

"I want to write a story for my paper," Dyer said, "and I want to know if you're quitting."

"Just shut up, you old bastard, and stay out of my way."

"Don't you curse me."

"Look, Dyer, I've had enough of your crap for three years. You've been ripping me ever since I got here. I won't put up with it anymore. Stay the hell away from me. If you ever come within two feet of me again, I'll put your face in the toilet bowl and flush it."

"You're a gutless son of a bitch. Let's see you do it. I'll be right up."

"You do that. You come up here and I flush your damn head in the toilet bowl."

Chance and Belinsky sat on the bed and talked for ten minutes. Nobody came. Chance started the water for a bath. Bo called the front desk and ordered all calls stopped until noon. He put the "Do Not Disturb" sign on the door.

The disturbance followed. Dyer reached the players' room, loosened his tie and removed his jacket, hanging it on the doorknob of the next-door room. Chance was in the bath, and Belinsky was brushing his teeth when they heard the knock. Bo walked to the door carrying the cup of water he had been using to brush his teeth.

Belinsky later told the media that Dyer stepped into the room and said, "Now, you gutless son of a bitch, let's see you put my head in the toilet bowl."

The following exchange ensued, according to Bo:

"For crissakes, Braven, go back to your room and sober up."

"Go ahead, tough guy, let's see you put me on my ass, let's see you."

Dyer, according to Belinsky, pushed his way into the room, his chest against Bo's. "I didn't want to have to hit him," Bo said. "I threw the glass of water at him, hoping it would sober him up and make him leave."

Instead, Bo continued, Dyer reached down into Belinsky's attaché case, pulled out a bottle of hair tonic and swung it at Bo, the bottle grazing his face.

"It was at that point," Belinsky said, "that I flattened him with my left hand."

Said Dyer, "It was Bo who initiated the phone calls. He had found out that I had written he was quitting and he wanted me to change the story. I told him it was too late and he told me he was going to stick my head in the toilet. He called me a nasty name. I wasn't going to take that and I went to his room. We argued for a couple of minutes and I turned to look for Dean. It was at that moment he hit me. I never reached for a bottle of shaving cream and I never held a grudge against him. The whole thing would have been forgotten if he had been man enough to apologize."

Bo's punch landed on Dyer's right ear. The reporter fell backward, his head slamming against the wall. His mouth was open, his eyes shut and blood covered his face as he lay propped slightly against the wall.

Chance called trainer Freddie Frederico, who called Rigney. Both rushed to the room.

"I thought Braven was dead," Rigney recalled. "I turned to

Bo and Dean and told them that I didn't want to hear their lies."

Dyer was revived with smelling salts and sent to the hospital for x-rays that proved negative and for treatment of the cuts.

Rigney called Haney and then informed Bo that he was being suspended without pay. He told Bo that the club would return him to Los Angeles and then contact him shortly.

Bo was angry. He believed that Rigney wasn't interested in his side, didn't care why Dyer had come to *his* room, and was so determined to get him off the team that he wouldn't even ask Chance what had happened.

"I was sick," Bo said. "I felt like I was just about to hit the big money. I felt like I was just learning how to pitch, to win in the major leagues. I was on the verge of becoming a big star, and now here I was, guilty without a trial."

Bo left with a 9-8 record and 2.87 ERA. "I was pitching as well as Dean at that point," he said, "and Dean went on to win the Cy Young Award. I'd have gone on to win 15 or 18 games. The Angels hurt me, but they hurt themselves even more."

A week passed while Bo and his attorney, Paul Caruso, studied their options. The Angels then announced they were optioning Bo to Hawaii, additionally angering him. "I'm their best pitcher," he said. "How can they ship me out?"

The Angels decided on the move as a means of countering possible litigation had Bo remained on the suspended list. Bo and Caruso went to New York in a futile attempt to meet with Commissioner Ford Frick, who in the grand tradition of the game said only that it was a club matter.

Bo had a last fling with his Hollywood friends and headed for Hawaii, determined to relax and enjoy it, certain that he was through as a ballplayer.

The Angels, however, weren't high on the idea of Bo simply becoming a beach bum. It wasn't that they were particularly concerned about what happened to him, but rather that they didn't want to lose a 27-year-old left-hander without getting anything in return.

Thus, on the last day of the winter meetings in December, they announced Belinsky had been traded to Philadelphia for first baseman Costen Shockley and pitcher Rudy May.

It was the end of one chapter, the start of another. Philadelphia, Houston, Pittsburgh, St. Louis, Cincinnati. A total of eight more wins and a string of empty bottles, empty hopes. Along the way a marriage that didn't work, to former *Playboy* centerfold Jo Collins, the mother of his son, Stevie. Since then, another failed marriage, this to a Weyerhaeuser (the paper people) heiress he met by rescuing her from the surf in Hawaii.

Now Bo is again living in Hollywood, but it is not like it once was. He is a rehabilitated alcoholic and his nights are spent in speaking engagements on behalf of the program to which he submitted himself.

His former roomie, Ohio farmboy Dean Chance, won 20 games again for Minnesota in 1967, held out for a $60,000 contract the next spring, injured his back rushing to get in shape and was never the same pitcher while also performing for the New York Mets and Detroit Tigers in a career that extended through the 1971 season. Chance now manages several touring carnival shows, having also briefly managed heavyweight contender Earnie Shavers.

Regrets? Neither has any.

"I had my moments and I have my memories," Belinsky said. "If I had the attitude about life then that I have now, I'd have done a lot of things differently. But you make your rules and you play by them. I knew the bills would come due eventually, and I knew I wouldn't be able to cover them."

Chapter
VI

THE BILLS were a long way from coming due when Belinsky got off to his 5-0 start in 1962, providing much of the early impetus as the Angels fashioned one of the most remarkable seasons ever by a young expansion team.

The mood and style were actually established late in spring training when the Dodgers, flying west from their Florida training base for the season opener in the new stadium at Chavez Ravine, stopped in Palm Springs to play the first of what was expected to become an annual series of exhibition games with the Angels.

The Angels would come from behind to win in 35 games that year, 18 in their last at-bat, and they set the tone on April 2 before an overflow crowd at the Polo Grounds by winning the "City Championship" via a 6–5 victory over the confident Dodgers. Albie Pearson hit a three-run homer off the Dodgers' money pitcher, Johnny Podres, to tie the game in the eighth, and Joe Koppe singled in the winning run off Pete Richert in the ninth.

The teams met twice before the start of the 1963 season and twice before the start of the 1964 season, with the Angels stretching their winning streak to five before the embarrassed Dodgers temporarily bowed out of the series. It would be divulged later that owner Walter O'Malley was simply embarrassed over his club's inability to beat the Angels and also angered by the Angels' plan to end their tenancy at Dodger Stadium in favor of constructing their own home in Anaheim.

The then Dodgers' general manager, Buzzie Bavasi, said it was impractical for a club that trained in Florida to fly to California for a preseason exhibition game and then fly east again to open the season.

The two teams would not meet again until 1969, when the Dodgers ended the five-game losing streak by beating the Angels at Anaheim Stadium. They have met annually ever since with the standings through 1980 being a more realistic 17-15-1, the edge belonging still to the Angels. It is now known as a Freeway Series with the three games divided between Los Angeles and Anaheim.

In 1962, all freeways led to the Dodgers' magnificent new stadium only a few miles from City Hall, where much politicking had been done before O'Malley finally was able to build his dream house, overcoming the opposition of a public referendum based on the contention that the city was simply giving away valuable land. The Dodgers and their stadium eventually played a significant role in the downtown renaissance, and it's unlikely today anyone would criticize that long-ago transaction.

At the time, however, there was much criticism, and O'Malley looked for financial and vocal support from any source. Among those who provided it was Gene Autry, whose station, it will be recalled, had broadcast the Dodgers' games.

Now Autry's station broadcast the games of another team, Autry's team, a team Autry and O'Malley had committed to playing in the new stadium on the very night that the franchise was awarded. The Angels drew 1,144,063 in their first season in O'Malley's stadium, almost double what they had drawn in Wrigley Field.

The Dodgers enjoyed a housewarming to end all housewarmings, drawing 2,755,184, still the sixth highest single-season attendance total ever. Ultimately, the Dodgers' shadow would prove suffocating, but in 1962, at least, coexistence seemed possible. The Angels' improbable success on the field kept the turnstiles humming, particularly when the Yankees were in town.

A three-game series with New York in June attracted 146,623, including Marilyn Monroe. Miss Monroe made a presentation before the first game. "You'll do it at home plate," a club official said. "Where's that?" Monroe asked.

The Yankees attracted more than 120,000 for each of their two ensuing visits to Dodger Stadium. They looked forward to it as much as the fans did. Johnny Grant, a disc jockey then for Autry's KMPC, held nightly parties for the Yankees at his San Fernando Valley home. Some of Hollywood's loveliest starlets attended. The parties seldom ended before dawn, and the Yankees seldom looked quite as fierce the next night. Grant would never confirm a theory that Autry was the secret sponsor of those parties.

This, however, was the one year the Angels didn't really need that kind of help. Years later, Eli Grba would say the camaraderie of that summer would stay with him always. Fueled by characters such as Ryne Duren, Art Fowler and Leon Wagner, the Angels rode a spiritual high, a bus that came to be known as Desire.

Autry and Leonard Firestone found out about it when they took the team bus to the airport in Washington, D.C. An East Coast air defense test delayed the Angels' flight, and the team spent several hours in Duke Ziebert's restaurant, depleting Duke's beer and wine supply. They were headed for a four-game September series in Yankee Stadium, the pennant on the line, but you would never have known it. The players made Autry and Firestone sit in the back of the bus and subjected them to the blackest of gallows humor, a trademark during a season in which the club's press corps continually wrote about the bus rides.

Loose?

"If we win this thing," Rigney said at one point, "they might have to cancel the World Series because they'll never be able to find all my players after the pennant celebration.''

In the type of hijinx that characterized the season, Rigney once called on Earl Averill to pinch-hit, and Averill raced to the bat rack, tore off his jacket and ran onto the field wearing a football jersey.

Fowler and Duren sharpened an Abbott and Costello routine and were featured in every cocktail lounge in the American League. Duren seldom stopped when the lounges closed. He paraded up and down the corridor of a Baltimore hotel one night, looking for someone to drink with. Finally, concerned that the noise would attract security, Grba, wearing only shorts, emerged from his room and flattened Duren with a solid right. He then hoisted the relief pitcher over his shoulder and carried him down five flights, depositing him in his own room. It was one of the few times starter Grba was credited with a save on behalf of reliever Duren.

Rigney, who displayed a Midas touch throughout the season, emerged as the American League's Manager of the Year. Fred Haney was named Executive of the Year. Billy Moran was the All-Star second baseman, and Leon Wagner the All-Star right fielder and Player of the Game in the second of the then two All-Star games. Wags hit his club record 37 homers that year and drove in 107 runs. The leading hitter was a 20-year-old shortstop named Jim Fregosi, who played the final 58 games after being recalled from Dallas–Fort Worth to replace Joe Koppe.

That spring, Tom Sheehan, a veteran Giants scout, had stood next to Rigney during an Angels workout in Palm Springs and asked, ''Who's the kid at short?''

''Fregosi,'' Rigney replied. ''Jim Fregosi. We drafted him from Boston and he's going to be a great one.''

''Don't be ridiculous,'' Sheehan said. ''You can find shortstops like him under every rock in Arizona.'' Sheehan would eventually apologize, admitting to Rigney he had made a mistake.

Fregosi, a state broad-jump champion and winner of 11 letters at Serra High School in San Mateo, California, ultimately retired in possession of virtually every Angels offensive record, having appeared in six All-Star games. He was Rigney's favorite and Autry's favorite, the team leader on the field and the manager when the Angels ended 19 years of frustration by winning their first title.

Fregosi had been selected in the expansion draft because the Angels were fortunate to have the Giants and Dodgers scouting reports, the information that also led them to draft Dean Chance and Bob Rodgers, among others.

Chance was 14-10 in his rookie season, performing as both starter and reliever, the leading winner on a staff that also featured Ken McBride (11-5), the irrepressible Bo (10-11) and a relief corps whose ranks were deeper, perhaps, than any ever since. The bullpen required reservations, what with Duren, Fowler, Morgan, Jack Spring and Dan Osinski fighting for front row seats. Rigney used them all. In future years he would develop a reputation as a Captain Hook, the label applied to all managers who are quick to yank their starting pitchers. In 1962, he had no choice.

The rules governing the allocating of a save were stricter then, and yet Duren had 9, Morgan and Fowler 7 each, and Spring 6. Osinski arrived late in the year, the man for whom Belinsky was originally to be traded.

Osinski was a 6-1, 195-pound Pole from Chicago, one of the more powerful players ever to perform for the Angels. He proved it during an end-of-the-year party on the road, picking up rotund sportswriter Bud Tucker and dangling him out the window of a 15th-floor hotel suite by his heels.

"I was afraid," Tucker would say later, "someone would hand Osinski a drink, and he would simply turn and reach for it."

Bob Rodgers hailed from Prospect, Ohio, and immediately became the "Prospect from Prospect." He caught 155 games that year, breaking the American League's rookie record of 133 set by the legendary Mickey Cochrane in 1925. Rodgers batted .258, drove in 61 runs and was second to Tom Tresh in balloting for the Rookie of the Year Award. He and Fregosi also began to lay the groundwork for their managerial careers, spending countless hours in countless coffee shops with Rigney, delving into the managerial textbook, acquiring the tools that would allow them to play with intelligence and later become managers themselves, Fregosi with the Angels and Rodgers with the Milwaukee Brewers.

The Angels passed their 1961 victory total on August 19 of 1962 and finished the season 86-76, 10 games behind the Yankees and 5 behind the third-place Minnesota Twins. A double-header sweep of Washington had brought the second-year Angels back to Los Angeles on July 4 in first place. Owners Autry and Reynolds were among the 3,000 fans who greeted them at the airport. A headline written by Mal Florence in the morning *Times* read: "Heaven Can Wait! Angels in 1st on 4th."

And they might have stayed there, the magical blend of prospects and rejects, young and old, scoring the most improbable pennant victory ever, if it hadn't been for three freak injuries of the type that has haunted the club throughout its history.

It was in early April that outfielder Hunt, who had driven in 84 runs and slugged 25 homers the year before, broke his collarbone while flexing a bat behind his shoulders prior to a plate appearance. Hunt did not play again until late September, ending the season with only one home run and one RBI. Hunt was limited to 59 games the next year and forced to retire at 30.

The consistent hitting of Wagner, Moran and Lee Thomas compensated some for Hunt's loss, helping to keep the Angels in the race until the devastating loss of Fowler and McBride on consecutive days in early August.

Fowler went down first, nailed by a line drive off the bat of Ed Sadowski during pregame practice in Boston on August 6. The 40-year-old relief pitcher required nine stitches to close a cut above his left eye. He reclined in the trainer's room and said, "I thought it was my arm. Don't worry, Rig. I'll be back tomorrow."

Fowler lost the sight in his left eye and there were no tomorrows for him—at least that year. He appeared in 59 games in 1963, and was still getting minor league hitters out in his late 40s. But the accident in Boston had deprived him of the assuredness that was his trademark, the ability to throw strikes as if blessed with radar.

Fowler would long ponder the irony of the accident. It happened while he was walking across the outfield, where he was seldom found. Fowler loathed the pregame running drills and employed any excuse to get out of them.

"I've never seen a guy win 20 games by running the ball to the plate," he said frequently.

He couldn't find an excuse on August 6 and was headed back to the dugout when the accident occurred.

The next day, McBride, who had earlier won 10 straight games, was discovered to have a cracked rib, the apparent result of a prolonged bout with pleurisy. The doctors said McBride would be out only two weeks. It was closer to six. The ace of the staff had only one decision over the final six weeks and that was a loss.

Nevertheless, the Angels were still only 4½ games behind when they went to Yankee Stadium for a Labor Day doubleheader that drew 55,705, the largest crowd to have yet seen the Angels play. The Yankees won the opener, 8–2, and were ahead, 5–0, after seven innings of the second game. The Angels bubble seemed ready to burst. But Albie Pearson hit a two-run homer in the eighth and the Angels scored four in the ninth to salvage a 6–5 win.

They continued to play with persistence the next night, rallying from a 4–0 deficit to again defeat the Yankees, 7–6, and close to within 3½ games.

A 6–5 loss in the series finale made it a deficit of 4½ games again, but two wins in an ensuing three-game series at Baltimore and a two-game shutout sweep engineered by Chance (with a one-hitter in which Fregosi hit his first major league homer) and Grba at Minnesota enabled the Angels to return for their final home stand trailing by only 4.

Inexplicably, it was at this point that the miracle expired. The Angels lost six in a row to Kansas City, Detroit and Baltimore. They won only 4 of the final 16 games. The Bus Named Desire was at last stalled, finally on empty, but hardly, it seemed, an outdated model in need of major overhaul.

And yet it would be several years before the Angels were again a factor in the pennant race, the surprising success of 1962 slowly taking on the appearance of a fluke rather than what it was, what it should have been, a springboard to bigger and better years.

The mistake the owners had made in withdrawing their profits after the 1961 season was compounded when they and others saw more to the 1962 success than was there, believing that since it had come so easily, why pour money into the farm system? They made a waiver deal here, a minor league acquisition there, a patchwork approach to a patchwork team.

"In its final form," co-owner Robert Reynolds said years later, "the effect of 1962 was harmful. From top to bottom, we overestimated what we had and what we had to do. We were lulled into a false sense of security."

Chapter

VII

ROOMING TOGETHER in their first spring with the Angels, Rick Reichardt and Tom Egan came to be known as The Millionaires Club.

Reichardt, a 21-year-old outfielder from the University of Wisconsin, and Egan, an 18-year-old catcher from Rancho High in Whittier, California, were two of the nation's most coveted athletes among those eligible to be signed in June of 1964.

This was at a time when any amateur free agent was fair game for any club, when the introduction of the free agent draft was still a year away. Both Reichardt and Egan received bonus offers from all 20 teams. Egan's choice was complicated by offers of more than a hundred college football scholarships, his work as a Rancho quarterback having attracted national attention.

Both signed with the Angels. Egan received a bonus of $100,000. Reichardt got $200,000, the largest signing bonus to that time and still among the largest ever received by an amateur free agent.

Gene Autry, who personally led the hunt for both men, noted that the Reichardt bonus was more than the studios used to budget for one of his movies and far more than the star generally received.

"As soon as I hand him the check," Autry said, "I'm going to ask for a loan."

The benefits the Angels hoped to accrue from their investments never materialized. Reichardt retired at 30, having spent only three and a half seasons with the Angels and six and a half as a major leaguer. Egan also retired at 30, having never been anything except an irregular for either the Angels or White Sox.

Both players were victims of the type of physical misfortune that has had Autry shaking his head for 20 years. Both represented the frustrations of a farm system that has continuously experienced difficulty in producing quality talent, never really rebounding from the owners' initial decision to withdraw their 1961 profits and the "false sense of security" created by the success of 1962.

The numbers tell some of the story. In the years from 1961 through 1979, the Angels signed 956 high school and college free agents. Of these, 98 played at least one inning in the majors, a pathetic percentage of .103. And of the 98, only 30, giving the Angels the best of it, had or are having careers noted in some measure for length and/or accomplishment.

Examples: outfielder Jay Johnstone (class of '63), pitcher Tom Burgmeier ('64), first baseman Jim Spencer ('65), third baseman Aurelio Rodriguez ('65) and pitcher Marty Pattin ('65) were all still active in 1980, although none with the Angels and none in a position to say his had been the career of a superstar.

There have been no superstars, illustrated by the fact that until 1979, when Willie Aikens hit 21 homers and drove in 81, the Angels had never had one of their own hit 20 homers and drive in 80 runs in a season.

The strength, so to speak, has been in the area of pitching. The Angels have produced three 20-game winners (Clyde

Wright, Andy Messersmith and Frank Tanana) and a number of reasonably successful relief pitchers (Burgmeier, Minnie Rojas, Ken Tatum, Dave LaRoche, Tom Murphy, Andy Hassler and Sid Monge, among them).

Yet Tanana, signed in 1971, was the last farm product to gain a regular berth in the rotation. And the 1979 division winner had only three home-growns in the regular lineup: third baseman Carney Lansford (the best all-around player yet produced by the Angels), shortstop Jim Anderson (who appeared in just 96 games) and the aforementioned Aikens, who was used both at first base and as a designated hitter.

When the 1980 team, intent on defending its division title, was hit by a severe injury wave, the farm system was unable to respond, the cupboard being characteristically bare.

"This organization," one of the Angels' top scouts said in a 1968 interview with the *Long Beach Independent,* "has never had a firm conviction, a firm belief, that the way to build a successful team is through the scouting and farm system. It has never been able to shake the mentality that developed after the 1962 season. Everyone, from top to bottom, thought it would be so easy. They're paying a price now, and they'll continue to pay it for many years."

Some said it was the only thing the Angels seemed willing to pay for, but the truth is, it's that way with an expansion team. The job is tougher, the criticism easier. There are more holes to fill, more pressure to force-feed young players who aren't ready for the majors, more pressure on young players who are asked to carry clubs devoid of the type of veterans who can do it. It generally takes five years for a farm system to start producing, a long wait for impatient fans, media and owners.

The frustration was increased in the case of the Angels, since they seemed to have the opportunity to make it a shorter wait. They seemed to have a lot going for them.

This was baseball's first expansion and the talent wasn't diluted to the extent it now is. The free agent draft wasn't initiated until 1965, meaning the Angels had four years to mine the talent-rich southern California area, their home base. And, as a new team, the Angels offered a quicker route to the majors, a shorter wait for youngsters who might be backed up and lost in organizations such as the Yankees and Dodgers.

The opportunity was squandered. The Angels failed to take advantage of what seemed available in their own backyard. They signed 289 college and high school free agents in a sweeping bid to man their new farm clubs through those first four years, but only three or four ever had any real impact on the Angels.

Jim McGlothlin, signed in 1961, pitched successfully for several seasons and was traded in 1969 for the controversial Alex Johnson. Tom Satriano and Paul Schaal, both signed in 1961, gave some early solidarity to the infield. Ed Kirkpatrick (1962) and Jay Johnstone (1963) fashioned long careers but had their best years with other teams, both leaving in trades that proved less than memorable for the Angels.

"Haney's approach," said an Angel scout, "was based on quantity. He'd spend $100,000 to sign ten players, but he hated the idea of giving it all to one. He came from the old school and had difficulty coming to grips with the idea of big signing bonuses. He believed in numbers alone there was always the chance of finding that diamond in the rough."

While area scouts such as Tuffie Hashem and Rosey Gilhousen were considered among baseball's best, it was impossible for them to be everywhere. The Angels, seldom (at least initially) outhustled on the field, were clearly outhustled off it.

In addition, that important and formulative period was clouded by whispers that the Angels were reluctant to sign black players, a contention the club frequently and vehemently denied but was impossible to substantiate, since the minuscule number of blacks signed by the farm system over the years almost took on the appearance of tokenism.

The Angels never seemed hesitant to employ black or Latin players—Leon Wagner, Jose Cardenal, Vic Power, Felix Torres, Chuck Hinton, Bubba Morton, Alex Johnson, Bobby Bonds, Don Baylor, Rod Carew and Dan Ford among them—but most were acquired by other means.

In 20 years, only 24 black players have come out of the Angels' farm system to play an inning or more in the majors, and only Ken Landreaux, Willie Aikens, Thad Bosley and Ron

Jackson, all signed since 1971, have done so with any real success. In the four years before the introduction of the 1965 draft, the Angels signed only one black (outfielder Dick Simpson) who would later spend more than a day or two with the varsity.

Rosey Gilhousen, the respected scout now employed by the Kansas City Royals, said, "At no time with the Angels was I told not to sign black players. I never heard any of our other scouts say they were either. Yet there did seem to be some feeling in the black community that the Angels weren't the club for them. I don't know where or how it started—maybe another organization spreading the rumor—but it got to be frustrating because we would continually outbid other clubs for a black player only to see him sign elsewhere for the lesser money. We lost some good players because of it."

The Angels, of course, were bucking the Dodgers, the team that had opened the major league door to black players, the team that employed such celebrated blacks during the 1960s as Maury Wills, Jim Gilliam, Charlie Neal, John Roseboro, Lou Johnson, Willie Davis and Tommy Davis.

The Dodgers' shadow engulfed the Angels on and off the field, compounding the frustrations of farm director Roland Hemond, who said, "It was very difficult establishing an identity. We were second fiddle to the Dodgers in every regard. Our scouts not only had to introduce themselves, they had to explain who the Angels were."

The major successes were at the minor league level. Operating frequently with limited funds and on the patchwork philosophy that followed the 1962 success, the club's scouts scoured the minors to effectively plug holes the system couldn't keep plugged, helping the Angels win 80 or more games four times in the first seven years. Billy Moran, Joe Koppe, Felix Torres, Bob Lee, Minnie Rojas, Bo Belinsky and Aurelio Rodriguez were among the minor league players acquired via draft, trade or purchase, the veteran executive, Marvin Milkes, providing significant insights and connections.

Rigney called Milkes his special weapon. He would soon need others, since the stopgap approach adopted by all expansion clubs was never designed as a panacea. The Angels' inability to construct a foundation during those early years was compounded later when Autry established a revolving door to the front office and Haney, who retired after the 1968 season, was followed by Dick Walsh, Harry Dalton and Buzzie Bavasi, three changes within an eight-year span, each new man bringing in a new farm director, new scouts and new philosophy.

Walsh replaced Haney and attempted to streamline the scouting system, dismissing some scouts, reassigning others and placing the Angels in a scouting co-op with the Cubs, Braves and Yankees. Roland Hemond quit to become a vice president with the White Sox and was replaced by Tom Sommers, a former player in the Angels' system.

That system, Walsh said when he took over, was devoid of talent, a contention that definitely could not be questioned after Walsh finished negotiating a series of trades that stripped the organization of a number of talented players: Jay Johnstone, Tom Egan, Tom Bradley, Doug Griffin, Ken Tatum, Jarvis Tatum, Lloyd Allen, Jim Spencer, Rick Reichardt, Aurelio Rodriguez, Vern Geishert, Pedro Borbon, Jim McGlothlin, Tom Satriano, Bobby Knoop. Veterans and youngsters alike were all traded. There was no time for a five-year plan when they were competing with the Dodgers, Walsh said, adding "You've got to go for broke every year."

Walsh was fired at the end of the 1971 season, a few months after the club had enjoyed one of its most successful drafts ever, signing pitcher Frank Tanana, second baseman Jerry Remy and third baseman Ron Jackson, among others.

Harry Dalton, architect of the Baltimore dynasty, replaced Walsh and sang the same song, insisting there was nothing in the system. He brought in Walter Shannon, his scouting director at Baltimore, and a number of his key Baltimore scouts.

Dave Collins, Dave Chalk and Bruce Bochte were among the players drafted and signed in 1972. Julio Cruz and Thad Bosley were among those signed in 1974. Willie Aikens, Carney Lansford, Bobby Clark, Dickie Thon, Paul Hartzell and Dan Goodwin were among those signed in 1975. Ken Landreaux, a future .300 hitter for Minnesota, was signed in 1976.

Dalton believed he was on schedule, his bid to provide the

foundation that had long been missing enhanced by Autry's decision to approve the spending of $5 million on the signing of Joe Rudi, Don Baylor and Bobby Grich, all emancipated by the 1976 changes in the reserve system.

Autry disagreed. He apparently didn't believe Dalton was making the necessary progress. He surprisingly told a reporter years later that Dalton's development of a farm system had been lagging. Bavasi was hired as executive vice president and chief operating officer. It was late in the 1977 season, at a time when Dalton was still executive vice president and general manager, his initial five-year contract having been renewed. The Angels were again an organization of contradictions.

The owner wanted an improved farm system and yet told Bavasi to tighten the purse strings. Bavasi responded by telling Dalton to trim $400,000 from his player development budget. Dalton almost told Bavasi what he could do, but instead found a job as general manager of the Milwaukee Brewers, taking Shannon and his scouts with him. Then the man who was told to tighten the purse strings was given permission to continue the bid to buy a pennant.

The ensuing three seasons saw Bavasi spend $1 million for Jim Barr, $2.2 million for Lyman Bostock, $2.4 million for Bruce Kison and $4 million for Rod Carew. The farm system that Autry didn't think Dalton was developing fast enough provided Bavasi with sought-after trade material in Thad Bosley, Richard Dotson, Willie Aikens, Dan Goodwin, Ken Landreaux, Ron Jackson and Dave Engle, among others. Bavasi also reduced the number of farm clubs from five to four ("There weren't enough prospects to sustain five clubs"), the number of scouts from 21 to 12, the number of roving instructors to one (none his first year). Later, when the free agent philosophy had not delivered the anticipated results, Bavasi began to rebuild it all. But the 40-year baseball executive also said the game's economics had reached a point where most clubs would have to refine their priorities, placing an emphasis either on the reentry draft or the farm system.

In the Angels' case, the commitment to the farm system— be it on the part of the general manager or the owner—has always seemed questionable. Roland Hemond had doubts himself when the farm and scouting director went to co-owner Robert Reynolds in the spring of 1964. Hemond, exasperated at the club's failure to take a more affirmative approach to its farm system, told Reynolds that either this was the time to get more active or, perhaps, he was working for the wrong club.

Hemond told Reynolds that this seemed to be a key year with young talents such as Rick Reichardt, Tom Egan and Willie Crawford (who would ultimately sign with the Dodgers) available and that "If we're going to make strides we have to get more aggressive."

Reynolds agreed and authorized Hemond to begin an all-out pursuit of any or all of the three. Hemond called Autry and asked the former singing cowboy to lead the posse in search of the touted Wisconsin outfielder, Rick Reichardt, who would later say that the personal involvement of Autry and Reynolds was one reason he signed with the Angels.

Reichardt could have signed anywhere and, in fact, was offered considerably more by the Yankees and Kansas City As. The As' owner, Charles Finley, a man conditioned to getting his way, was told by the young player that he could offer $1 million and "I still won't sign because I want to play in an area like Los Angeles or New York."

Reichardt represented Jack Armstrong, the All-American boy. He was the son of a noted surgeon and a pre-med major himself. He was the only player in Big Ten history to lead the conference in batting for two consecutive years (.429 as a sophomore and .472 as a junior), and he was the Big Ten's leading receiver in 1963 as a star end on the Wisconsin football team that lost to USC in the Rose Bowl, 42–37. He was articulate and accessible and he said such things as:

—"My greatest fault is a lack of concentration. It's just that my mind is so active it's conditioned to think quickly of many things."

—"The game requires a crystallization of thought. It requires dedication, discipline and determination."

—"The winds were diametrically opposed."

—"The general jokes of the clubhouse" (Reichardt was frequently needled and criticized about his fielding) "don't bother me. Actually it's a healthy situation. I am concerned that sometimes a thing said in jest can be carried too far. We have a tendency to project our own inadequacies on others."

—"One or two shaky games are not indicative. It takes time and experience before you master the intricacies of each park."

Intricacies? Inadequacies? The Angels found it difficult to find any initially.

Reichardt was flown to Los Angeles for the signing ceremony and walloped four home runs during a special batting practice at Dodger Stadium. It was June 24, 1964.

"You think I wasn't impressed?" Bill Rigney said. "He hadn't had any sleep in 36 hours and all he does is rocket four balls out of here. The only other kid who impressed me that much was Willie Mays."

The bonus was part of Reichardt's burden. The comparisons were another. In the spring of 1966, Rigney said, "I'll be sincerely surprised if Reichardt isn't the American League's next superstar." A *Sporting News* headline read: "Rigney Sees Reichardt Cast in Mantle Mold." It was the spring of Reichardt's first full season with the club, and Reichardt soon showed that he just might be all of that.

He hit the Angels' first home run at Anaheim Stadium, teeing off against Tommy John, then of the Chicago White Sox. He hit two homers in the same inning of an April 30 game at Boston. He compiled an 11-game hitting streak and, by the All-Star break, was batting .288 with 16 homers and 44 RBI.

Unfortunately, he was also suffering severe headaches and periodic fainting spells. Reichardt saw a battery of doctors and was examined at the Mayo Clinic. The diagnosis was that a congenital blockage of the ureter had created high blood pressure of such severity that a kidney would have to be removed.

The operation was performed in midseason, and Reichardt did not return until the season's final game when he drew a standing ovation from an Anaheim Stadium crowd in a pinch-hitting appearance.

A year later, *The Sporting News* had a headline of another sort. It read: "Erratic Rick Tests Angels' Patience." And now Rigney was saying, "You can't play baseball and study the market at the same time. I want him to be a superstar and he can be. But he hasn't approached the job with the dedication it demands."

Reichardt hit 17 homers and drove in 69 runs in 1967. He led the Angels with 21 homers and 73 RBI in 1968. He had 13 homers and 68 RBI in 1969. His batting average in the years 1967 through 1970 fluctuated between .253 and .265. The statistics were those of a journeyman. Reichardt was again healthy, free of headaches and fainting spells, but it was as if some of the dedication, determination, discipline had been removed when his kidney was removed. A certain timidity replaced his customary aggressiveness. The drive was gone and Reichardt with it, the Angels believing Reichardt would get a return on his blue-chip investments before the blue-chip prospect fulfilled his celebrated potential.

Dick Walsh and his manager, Harold (Lefty) Phillips, traded Reichardt and third baseman Aurelio Rodriguez to Washington for third baseman Ken McMullen on April 26, 1970. Phillips, who spoke a language akin to Stengelese, couldn't communicate with Rodriguez, who spoke only Spanish. He also didn't understand a number of the things Reichardt said.

Reichardt spent one season with the Senators, two with the White Sox and retired to the field of insurance. Egan, his former partner in The Millionaires Club, the once coveted catcher, retired after the 1975 season, believing still if he'd ever gotten the opportunity to play regularly, if Earl Wilson hadn't broken his jaw with a 1969 fast ball, he would have lived up to the expectations.

That Egan and Reichardt never did is just one more reason the Angels' farm system has been left generally in need of repair.

Chapter

VIII

ONE OF the first visitors Gene Autry received after being awarded the franchise in St. Louis was Branch Rickey, former general manager of the Brooklyn Dodgers, an astute baseball thinker known as the "Mahatma."

Rickey congratulated Autry, wished him well and told him not to forget that aspect of the game's history which showed how difficult it was for two clubs to survive, to peacefully coexist, in the same stadium. Rickey employed as his examples the Browns and Cardinals in St. Louis, the Phillies and As in Philadelphia and the Red Sox and Braves in Boston.

"I advise you to get out from under as soon as you can," he said. "It just doesn't work."

This was 1961, a year before the Angels would move into Dodger Stadium. The new team had yet to play its first game. There were other problems to be attended to, and Autry didn't have to be told about the largest obstacle of all. He was aware of what happened in St. Louis and Philadelphia and Boston, and he was aware from that first night in Walter O'Malley's suite, when the details of the Dodger Stadium lease were hammered out, that it would be difficult merely surviving in the same city as the Dodgers, let alone the same stadium.

He knew that a search for a new, permanent home would have to be initiated early and that he didn't have the resources to build his own stadium, that he would have to have municipal help. He also knew he had no alternative but to move in with O'Malley, who was without alternatives himself.

In future years, long after the Angels had gone elsewhere in search of their identity, O'Malley's associates would confide that their boss had never really wanted the Angels as a roommate in his dream house, nor to provide another club with that kind of stepping-stone to the potential riches of Los Angeles. O'Malley, they said, was pressured into it, knowing that to demand $350,000 in territorial indemnification and then to force the new club out onto the street would be to risk arousing public animosity toward the Dodgers, who were still trying to heal the wounds stemming from the referendum, and risk arousing public sentiment on behalf of the Angels, who carried a name long familiar to Los Angeles fans.

That name, Angels, actually belonged to the Dodgers at the time Autry was awarded the franchise, since the Dodgers had purchased Wrigley Field and the minor league club as a first step in moving to Los Angeles. That the Angels simply usurped the name without asking permission was one more thing eating at O'Malley.

Instead, he appeared to roll out the red carpet, on which Autry trudged hesitantly, knowing that to remain amid the limited seating capacity of Wrigley Field for more than a year was to risk the loss of significant revenue and that he had no choice but to risk the permanent loss of his club's identity by becoming a tenant of O'Malley's.

Four years later, on the eve of the club's move to Anaheim, Robert Reynolds said all their fears had come true, and now the Angels had no alternative but to get out.

"We are like a boxer whose hands are tied," Reynolds said. "We have not been able to get out of our corner in the fight for the baseball dollar.

"We have been restricted in areas of promotions, merchandising, pay-TV and sponsors. We play in a park that advertises Union Oil and one of our sponsors is Standard Oil. We are cast under the Dodgers' shadow as long as we remain in Chavez Ravine."

At that point, after four years in Dodger Stadium, the Angels showed an approximate operating loss of $1.7 million, including $700,000 in the lame-duck season of 1965. The Dodgers were attracting 2 million annually, including more stars than attend an Oscars ceremony. The Angels had only Mamie Van Doren.

Attendance, falling at a pace comparable with the Angels' artistry, had dwindled from the 1,144,063 of 1962 to 821,015 in 1963, to 760,439 in 1964 and to 566,727 in 1965.

Only 945 fans turned out for the last day game the Angels played at Dodger Stadium, and one player said, "We're getting out of here just in time. I can't even give my passes away anymore."

Even Bo Belinsky knew it would come to that, though he learned his lesson the hard way. Bo, having been recently recalled from Hawaii in 1963 and scheduled to make his first start against Baltimore, said, "If I don't draw 15,000, they should send me right back to Hawaii."

Bo had drawn at least 12,000 for each of his starts on the island, but he failed to consider that this was a Thursday afternoon in late September, the Angels were in ninth place and he wasn't exactly the prodigal having returned. Bo pitched a five-hit, complete-game victory, but only 476 fans, the all-time smallest crowd at Dodger Stadium, where 30,000 annually turn out to see a spring exhibition game between the Dodgers and USC, were on hand.

"I wouldn't be so upset about it," Bo said later, "but it was obvious I wouldn't even have gotten 476 if 200 or so hadn't wanted to come out and boo me. What sadists."

Bo had been traded by the time the Angels decided against renewing an option that would have kept them in Dodger Stadium through the 1968 season, at which time, had they maintained the attendance pace, they would have been drawing about 100,000 annually and Autry would have long since hocked the saddles. "I couldn't have even interested my own station in the games," he said.

Approximately one month before expiration of that option clause, in the spring of 1964, the Angels notified O'Malley of their intention to move. The original agreement tied the Angels to Dodger Stadium for four years with an opportunity to stay for three more. Autry agreed to pay 7.5% of his attendance gross in rent. The Dodgers took all of the parking revenue and 50% of the concession gross. O'Malley even insisted on a clause by which the Angels, who televised 20 regular-season road games, would have to compensate the Dodgers for the loss those telecasts created at Dodger Stadium. And if the Angels ultimately became interested in pay-TV, it could only be through the pay-TV company O'Malley was at the time developing.

"Every department head in the Dodger organization," O'Malley said when the Angels moved in, "is available to help the new club. There will be no sabotage, no sniping. It's our desire they be successful. It's rare when a young married couple can move in with their in-laws and be happy. But this may be one of those rare occasions."

"They dollared us to death," Autry said later.

Amateur horticulturist O'Malley sent the Angels a bill for half the stadium's landscaping, a considerable sum since there was a considerable area to be landscaped. The Angels complained, arguing that the plants weren't going to be uprooted and replanted each time the Angels left town, that the Dodgers were going to landscape the stadium no matter how many tenants they had.

The Angels received a bill for window cleaning and again promptly complained, pointing out that the only windows were in the Dodgers' offices.

The Angels received a bill for the resurfacing and striping of the parking lot. They filed another complaint, suggesting that since they received no revenue from parking, they shouldn't be expected to pay for parking improvements.

The Angels were billed for half a season's supply of toiletries. They angrily complained again, saying the bill should be prorated on the basis of attendance, that no matter how bad a team the Angels were, the Dodgers still went through more toilet paper because of their greater attendance.

All of the complaints were arbitrated by the Dodgers' vice president in charge of saying no, Dick Walsh, a man who would later serve three seasons as general manager of the Angels, stirring up a storm of the type he was constantly responding to at Dodger Stadium. Walsh was a cold, efficient businessman who would be nicknamed "The Smiling Python" by the Angels' players while serving as their general manager. He had several shouting matches with the executives of both clubs then sharing Dodger Stadium, and there were many times that old friends Bavasi and Haney, the respective general managers, had to mediate the differences.

Nothing upset the Angels more than the location of their ticket office. While most of the club's executives worked out of a building in downtown Los Angeles, tickets were handled out of a windowless dungeon at Dodger Stadium. The office was in the left field corner, near the place where the groundskeeper kept his equipment. The only avenue for customers buying tickets in advance, for those interested in group purchases, took them past the towering manure piles, always a pleasant experience during the heat of summer or, in the words of a Dodger executive, the appropriate preparation for watching the Angels.

All of it served to put greater stress on the relationship and convince the Angels they would ultimately have to move. Autry knew it, and others sensed it. In the three years before the move to Anaheim was formally announced, the Angels received fifteen to twenty "feelers" from cities interested in calling the Angels their own.

Had the Angels been able to sustain their momentum of 1962, had management seen it for what it was instead of over-estimating its significance, had the club finished better than ninth, fifth and seventh in its next three years at Dodger Stadium and delayed or permanently forestalled the attendance skid, it is difficult to say whether the Angels would have picked up the option on the next three years at Dodger Stadium.

Even now, more than fifteen years later, Autry can't say, though he is doubtful anything could have convinced him coexistence was possible or that the Angels could have stayed anywhere in the metropolitan area and established their own credentials in the face of the Dodgers' enormous popularity.

He put business manager Cedric Tallis in charge of the relocation project and told Tallis that three points were essential. Autry wanted (1) to remain accessible to the Los Angeles market and to the areas of major growth; (2) to receive an appropriate lease that would give the Angels a share of both parking and concessions and in no way inhibit their involvement with television, including pay-TV; and (3) to have the type of stadium in which the fans were on top of the action, a stadium in which the seats were built as close as possible to the foul lines.

The first time Tallis got back to Autry was to inform him he would probably need a new car, since his old one was certain to disintegrate before he was through investigating all the propositions.

Ultimately a significant state of negotiation was reached, resulting in the 35-year lease that binds the Angels to Anaheim Stadium until 2001, at least. Anaheim became involved just after negotiations with the city of Long Beach collapsed, at a point when Tallis thought "all was lost."

Long Beach, 30 miles to the south of Los Angeles, a city believed to be home for more Iowans than Iowa itself and a city of considerable tidelands oil wealth, had invited Tallis to investigate its potential late in 1963. While restricted on the west by the Pacific Ocean, Long Beach offered an attendance market of about 4 million. It proposed the El Dorado Park area in the northeast section of the city as a possible stadium site, pointing out its proximity to several freeways.

Tallis was intrigued and so was Autry. The negotiations had almost reached the yes or no stage when two problems developed. The first was the possibility that Long Beach could not obtain tidelands money for an inland project. The city told the Angels not to worry, since the financing could be resolved. The second was that Long Beach insisted the club be called the Long Beach Angels. The Angels told the city to forget it, since under no circumstances would the club be called anything except Los Angeles or California.

Autry simply had been a corporate cowboy too long to underestimate the importance of Madison Avenue. He realized there was little chance of marketing the Long Beach Angels in New York, of selling it to potential radio sponsors. He had Tallis explain the club's predicament to Long Beach officials and tell them the club would not object if Long Beach was affixed to the name of the stadium.

The city remained firm, saying for all that money and all that land, it had a right to name the baby.

Among those watching and intrigued by the collapse in negotiations was a man named Rex Coons, a friendly and progressive mayor of the city of Anaheim, home of Disneyland but still known best for the Jack Benny routine in which Anaheim, Azusa and Cucamonga first came to prominence. The 1963 population of Anaheim was only 150,000, but there were 7 million people within a 50-mile radius. And the area, the county known as Orange, was exploding unlike any other in the country, the fruit and vegetable fields giving way to housing tracts and industrial developments at a dizzying pace. The per capita income was among the nation's highest and the politics among the most conservative.

The Angels were aware of Anaheim. Walt Disney had agreed to become a member of the club's new advisory board and had already suggested to Autry that the area should be explored. The Angels had also read a Stanford research study predicting a population belt from Santa Barbara to Mexico with Anaheim at the center. The Angels spent $23,000 on a study of their own and got the same information.

At about the same time in late 1963 that Tallis was telling Autry that Long Beach was out and that he'd have to start from scratch elsewhere, Rex Coons was knocking on his door. Coons also understood Long Beach was out, and he knew— or firmly believed—that a professional sports team was about the only thing Orange County was missing in its emergence from more than a century as a sleepy agricultural area, a pleasant spot for a resident of the Los Angeles complex to drive to on Sunday afternoon.

Coons had recently returned from Washington, D.C., where he and a hundred other Orange County politicians and businessmen had successfully petitioned the Bureau of the Budget to have Orange County designated a standard metropolitan statistical area, permitting its employment, economic and population figures, among others, to be listed separately rather than lumped with Los Angeles–Long Beach.

The trip to Washington had allowed Coons to thoroughly indoctrinate himself in the development of his and other counties, and he became convinced a professional sports team would be more than an additional impetus for the nation's fastest growing county, that it was the required frosting.

Coons, concerned that public knowledge would send land prices soaring and blow the deal before there was one, kept his convictions pretty much to himself. He told Bill Phillips, chairman of the Orange County board of supervisors, and he told Keith Murdoch, city manager in Anaheim; but until he received the Angels' informal approval, he acted independently of his city council, holding a number of clandestine meetings with Tallis and Reynolds. It was early 1964 and there was pressure on both the club and the city.

Coons realized he couldn't keep it quiet forever, and the Angels knew if they wanted their own stadium in 1966, if they didn't want to be trapped in Dodger Stadium until 1968, a decision had to be made soon. Coons and Phillips met with Tallis and Reynolds at the Los Angeles County Club.

"We have to know, Bob," Coons said.

"Does it matter what we call ourselves?" Reynolds asked.

"I don't give a damn," Coons said. "Why should I? I know every broadcast, every dateline will have Anaheim in it."

Reynolds gave his approval and a meeting was scheduled for Palm Springs in late March, at which time Anaheim would formally make its proposal to the Angels' board of directors.

A significant problem ensued—temporarily. A. J. Schute, senior member of the city council and the man who owned the land where Coons and Murdoch wanted to put the stadium, had by now learned what the land was to be used for and raised the price so drastically that Coons and Murdoch considered it beyond the city's reach. Ten days before the Palm Springs meeting, Anaheim had everything except the land on which to build a stadium.

The solution was offered by a man who insisted he communicated with God and had been working behind the scenes to prove Anaheim and the Angels were a match made in heaven. His name was C. J. Gill, a veteran real estate broker; he had gotten wind of the attempt to bring the Angels to Anaheim and of the problems with the original site.

"I'm a Christian Scientist," Gill recalled, "and I talked with the Supreme Being—it helps clear my mind—to seek His help in trying to determine the logical site for a stadium. I pray before any business deal—'If this be right for all, please let it happen.' I have a sound knowledge of Orange County real estate and as I prayed and reviewed the pieces of land, it came to me."

Gill envisioned a stadium on land then used for the growing of alfalfa, oranges and corn, a site, he would learn, that encompassed approximately 157 acres some two miles south of the original.

Did the Supreme Being tell Gil there was the possibility of a $150,000 commission if he was successful in getting the owners to agree to the sale of their land? That was never ascertained. What is certain is that Gill came to city manager Murdoch at the propitious moment, having put together the package that would cost the city approximately $4 million, in addition to a lifetime pass to the Angels' games, a bonus Herman Bruggeman insisted on when he committed his 21 acres of orange trees to the Gill package for $565,000.

Roland Reynolds paid for his own season tickets with the $1.3 million he received for his 70 acres of alfalfa. "A lot more fun than baling it," Bessie Reynolds said, watching a game at Anaheim Stadium years later.

The Angels filed their intention to move with the Anaheim City Council on April 9, 1964. The council and the board of supervisors met the next day, at which time the county officials, under pressure from conservative constituents such as R. C. Hoiles, publisher of the *Orange County Register,* backed out of the project, leaving the city of 150,000 to go it alone—"not at all afraid," as Coons said.

A nonprofit board was established to supervise negotiation of the contract with the Del Webb Construction Company, to prepare and handle the sale of private bonds to finance the project and to administer the 35-year lease with the city.

Architect Noble Herzberg was hired to design a stadium of approximately 50,000 seats. Autry and Tallis provided input in a bid to achieve the compact arena they envisioned. The groundbreaking was held in the middle of a cornfield on August 31, 1964. There were bands, balloons and all of the Disney characters, including Mickey Mouse, who presented Rigney. with a Disney pennant, the closest the Angels manager would get to holding the real thing.

The stadium itself was budgeted for $16 million and Webb brought it in for that, although concession and Stadium Club equipment raised the price to $24 million. The seating capacity was 43,204, which would be raised to about 70,000 when the Los Angeles Rams moved from the Memorial Coliseum in 1980. The impact of inflation can be measured by the fact that the construction of outfield seats and the enclosing of the stadium cost $30 million as compared with the original $24 million.

The move of the Rams also resulted in the moving of the stadium's most distinctive feature, the 230-foot-high Big A scoreboard, which cost $1 million and was financed by Standard Oil. The halo that rings the top of the Big A is flashed continuously after each Angels victory, but the club had never had to be concerned about complaints it is wasting electricity: there have never been that many victories.

Originally located behind the left field fence, the Big A now stands in a corner of the east parking lot, next to the Orange Freeway, one of several freeways that ring the stadium and make it accessible to more than 10 million people within a 50-mile radius.

The population and economic boom in Orange County had continued, enhancing a decision made fifteen years ago when it was all just starting, when Disney saw the potential that Walter Knott of Knott's Berry Farm had seen even many years before. (Berry Farm is a tremendous tourist attraction in southern California.)

The Angels' season ticket sales jumped from 2,600 to more than 5,000 in 1966, the first year in Anaheim, when the club finished sixth and drew 1,400,321, more than double the 1965 figure at Dodger Stadium. The Angels finished better than .500 only four times in the next thirteen years and yet failed to draw a million only four times—an impressive display of faith and patience by the partisans.

The quest for the first title, the division championship of 1979, generated a club record attendance of 2,523,575, a profit of $2.5 million and an ensuing season ticket sale of 17,562, an American League record.

Executive vice president Buzzie Bavasi, whose salary was based in part on increased attendance and decreased expenses, earned $328,000 in 1979, putting him in a class with some of the top executives of some of the leading corporations. But then there suddenly seemed plenty for everyone— at least on the basis of a potential not evident at Dodger Stadium.

The Dodgers had taken half the concessions and all the parking. The Anaheim Stadium lease permits the Angels to keep half the parking and two thirds of the concessions net. The club pays a minimum of $160,000 in rent or 7.5% of the admission gross up to $2 million, 10% after $2 million.

Gene Autry, wearing alligator boots and a tan suit cut in Western style, wielded the first shovel himself in 1964. His team still had two long years left in Dodger Stadium, two long years before Buzzie Bavasi, still with the Dodgers, presented the Angels with a cake that carried a frosted replica of Anaheim Stadium and the inscription "Good Luck." The Angels haven't always had that in Anaheim, but they have enjoyed a larger slice of income and identity, and their ticket office is out front at gate one, a long way from the groundskeeper's manure.

Chapter
IX

THE FINAL standings from 1963, 1964 and 1965 illustrate just how much of a lame duck the Angels were during their final three seasons in Dodger Stadium. The misleading euphoria of 1962 faded rapidly as the Angels finished ninth, fifth and seventh, their attendance falling from 821,015 to 760,439 to 566,727. A crowd of only 945 saw the Angels in their next-to-last game at Dodger Stadium, a 4–2 loss to Baltimore in an afternoon make-up of a rained-out night game.

"My players planned on this being a day off," the sarcastic Bill Rigney said, "and they can't adjust their thinking that quickly."

Rigney and Haney would no sooner plug one hole than there would be another somewhere else. One season it would be a lack of pitching, the next a lack of hitting. Bo Belinsky took a black Labrador retriever (the canine's name was Bimbo) with him to spring training in 1963, and it was soon being suggested that all the Angels had gone to the dogs.

A team that won 86 games while almost winning it all in 1962, the Angels won only 70 in 1963, won 82 in 1964, and won 75 in 1965. They finished 34 games behind the Yankees in 1963, were 17 behind the Yankees in 1964 and 27 behind Minnesota in 1965.

Rigney's ulcer put him in the hospital twice during the 1965 season, and a review of his quotes illustrates his frustration during the course of the three years:

—"This has to be a jack-up day. We've been playing defensively. We've been watching our pitches. We haven't been attacking."

—"It looks like it's even an effort for my players to swing the bat. It looks like they want a vacation."

—"We've been bluffing our way, going through the motions. If they'd really rather be somewhere else, we can accommodate them."

It became increasingly difficult to find substitutions on the waiver lists or in the minor league systems of other organizations. Impatience and frustration ate at the relationship between Haney and Rigney. The manager received a one-year extension at the end of the 1964 season and another at the end of the 1965 season, even though he was, at times, publicly second-guessed by Autry.

Haney, who some believed was left bitter and envious because of the acclaim Rigney received in the wake of the 1962 miracle, ultimately charged the press with an attempt to create a rift between himself and Rigney.

The situation was compounded by rumors that the Giants wanted Rigney to return as manager, a possibility that stimulated the prodigal in Rigney but never reached the point of a definitive offer. Finally, prior to a game on September 5, Haney held a press conference in Rigney's office and announced the one-year extension.

"Bill had no reason to say we haven't talked with him about the situation," Haney said emotionally. "And I said the same thing to his face, isn't that right, Bill?"

Rigney was about to respond when Haney continued, "I gave him my word three months ago that he would go to Anaheim as the manager. We hadn't had time to work out the details, but there's never been a question about it."

Rigney shrugged and smiled, wondering why, if there had never been a question about it, Autry had been quoted repeatedly during the previous week as saying a decision had not yet been made. But the manager bit his tongue. He was happy to be working and was committed to developing the Angels into a winner. Asked repeatedly over the years about his relationship with Haney, he would always answer the same: "Naturally two men working together are going to have their differences. Ours have never been that serious, and Fred has never second-guessed anything I've done on the field. A manager can't ask for anything more."

Which wasn't exactly true. Rigney kept asking for one more pitcher and/or one more hitter, a plea made by every manager of every team. The plea was more desperate in the case of the expansion Angels since there was no farm system to fill the gaps and little the Angels could offer in the way of trade bait.

Rigney went into the 1963 season saying the Angels were happy to accept the challenge of trying to prove that 1962 wasn't "a flash in the pan," saying, too, that "we improved 16 games last year and I'll be delighted to add 16 more."

He emerged saying that while it wasn't the most disappointing year he had ever experienced as a manager, "It certainly was the most frustrating. I had great expectations. I wasn't sure we could finish third again, but I was positive we could win 85 games again."

The magic that had produced 35 come-from-behind wins, 18 in the Angels' last at-bat, was gone. This time the Angels lost 28 games in the last at-bat and lost 60 of 106 games decided by three runs or less.

Mad Dog Thomas went down without even a whimper in 1963, batting .220 with 55 runs batted in after having hit .290 with 104 RBI the previous year. Bob Rodgers, the promising rookie catcher of 1962, was introduced to the realities of his position, suffering a broken finger early that year and later a sprained ankle. He caught only 99 games after catching the record 155 during the previous year and drove in 20 fewer runs. Leon Wagner, who still led the Angels with 26 homers and 90 RBI, drove in 17 fewer.

Albie Pearson became the first Angel to hit more than .300,

hitting .0004 more, but the inseparable Dean Chance and Bo Belinsky went from a combined 24-21 to a combined 15-27, and there was inconsistent relief pitching from the celebrated bullpen, of which the one-eyed Art Fowler became the ace almost by default, the renowned depth of 1962 having virtually disintegrated.

Rigney faced one of his toughest jobs of a tough season in spring training when he had to inform the 34-year-old Ryne Duren that he had been sold to Philadelphia. There was another tough task in May when an unhappy Eli Grba had to be told he was being farmed out.

"I just got married and I just bought a home," Grba said. "I don't understand how a guy can be good enough to pitch the opening game two years in a row and then isn't even good enough to pitch in the bullpen."

The old guard kept changing, and the burden fell on the 40-plus Fowler, who dismounted from one of the bicycles the Angels were forced to ride between their hotel and practice field in spring training and said, "A man my age should be excused from such nonsense. This kind of weather is more suited for Tom Collins—and I don't have the strength left to lift one."

The Angels got one of their few lifts in the season opener when Ken McBride pitched a four-hit, 4–1 victory. The club then scored just two runs in the next 21 innings, leaving 16 runners on base, to set the pattern for a season that ended with a 4–3 loss to Boston in which Felix Torres appropriately bunted into a triple play.

It was a season in which Haney complained that the Angels seemed to lack spirit and seemed to be interested only in individual pursuits.

The most individual of the Angels was again the left-hander named Belinsky, who announced in April that he was going on a health food diet prescribed by a veteran Los Angeles hippie named Gypsy Boots, who provided Bo with a daily supply of organic oranges. Mr. Boots regularly joined Miss Van Doren and Mr. Winchell in the dugout box seats at Dodger Stadium, producing a scene that was often more interesting than anything that transpired on the field.

Bo was optioned to Hawaii in May of 1963 and said he was considering applying for the voluntary retired list so that he could accept one of his many movie offers. The Angels quickly put Bo on the disqualified list, terminating his salary and influencing him to catch the next plane to Hawaii.

Mamie, at this time, received a call from Ray Johnson, owner of the Dallas–Fort Worth team of the Pacific Coast League. Johnson asked her if she would be willing to appear with Bo when the Islanders visited Texas.

"What are you willing to pay?" she asked.

"This is the minor leagues," Johnson replied.

"You may be the minor leagues but I'm the major leagues," Mamie said, terminating the proposal.

Bo ultimately returned, but appeared in just 13 games, losing 9 of 11 decisions, prompting his rejection of organic oranges in favor of his customary diet of wine, woman and song.

This was also the season in which the Angels signed another individual who tended to dance to his own music, outfielder Jim Piersall, then a veteran of 12 major-league summers. Piersall was 35 and had been released by the Mets because of a series of leg injuries and because the Mets' manager, Casey Stengel, hadn't laughed when Piersall ran the bases backward after hitting a home run.

A marvelously gifted player whose struggle with mental illness was chronicled in the book and movie, *Fear Strikes Out,* Piersall produced laughter and tears throughout his career. He had played for four other major league clubs and he said he was happy for the opportunity to join the Angels because he knew that next to Belinsky, Chance and Mad Dog Thomas, "I'd look sane."

Piersall spent three and a half years with the Angels, after which he briefly joined the club's promotions department. He won the Comeback of the Year Award for his .314 average in 1964 and he came back again in 1965 and 1966, making liars of the doctors who said he wouldn't play again after shattering a kneecap when he ran into the Dodger Stadium foul pole early in 1965.

"I can't sign a contract promising I'll stay within the lines of baseball as written by Abner Doubleday," Piersall said when he first signed with the Angels.

Two days later, Piersall proved it. He became embroiled in a pushing match with umpire Bill Kinnamon while zealously protesting a strike call. He was no sooner back in uniform than he was out of it, fined $250 and suspended four days.

Piersall called wife Mary to see if she had any advice. She told him to stay away from Mamie.

A year later, responding to Charles Finley's plan to book the Beatles into the Kansas City ball park, Piersall went to bat there wearing a Beatles wig.

"He can get me for a lot cheaper than the $150,000 he's giving those bums from Liverpool," Piersall said.

"OK," umpire Frank Umont told him, "I'll give you two minutes to do your act."

"Relax, Frank," Piersall said. "We're on national TV. I'll get you more camera time than you've ever had."

In August of 1963, pitcher Paul Foytack was tagged for four home runs in the same inning by Cleveland's Woodie Held, Pedro Ramos, Tito Francona and Larry Brown. It cost the Indians $350 to set off the center field fireworks after each blast, and publicity director Nate Wallick responded to the third of the four homers by telling the trigger man, "No more, we can't afford it."

Piersall greeted Foytack in the clubhouse later with earplugs and a stretcher.

The Angels limped out of the 1963 season and soon lost another familiar face, Leon Wagner being traded to Cleveland in a major winter transaction.

"I have nothing against Cleveland," Wagner said, "but I'd rather have been traded somewhere in the United States."

The Angels obtained pitcher Barry Latman and first baseman Joe Adcock, the imposing slugger who had been a catalyst in the pennants Haney won as manager of the Milwaukee Braves.

"I already have an assignment for Adcock," Rigney said at the time of the trade. "The big guy will room with Chance, and Joe will keep the only key."

Adcock was 37 at the time of the trade and conceded that

his best years were behind him. Nevertheless, he led the Angels with 21 homers in 1964, hit another 14 in 1965 and led the Angels again in 1966 with 18 homers and a .273 batting average.

He was the conscience of the clubhouse, a fundamentalist whose drive for perfection plagued his one attempt at managing, which was with the Cleveland Indians in 1967. Adcock retired then to his quarterhorse ranch in Coushatta, Louisiana.

Latman had a brief and unsuccessful tenure with the Angels, but did not have to worry about his future. He was the son-in-law of Leon Schwab, who owned the Hollywood drugstore of the same name, the place where Lana Turner and other actresses were allegedly discovered.

Latman was 6-10 in 1964, another desultory season highlighted only by the one-hitter that Ken McBride and Julio Navarro combined on in the Presidential opener in Washington, D.C., the marvelous pitching of Cy Young Award winner Dean Chance, a club record 11-game win streak in June, the all-around fine play of All-Star Jim Fregosi (18 homers, 72 RBI and a .277 batting average), the arrival of relief ace Bob Lee and the departure of veterans Lee Thomas and Billy Moran.

Thomas was traded in early June for Boston outfielder Lou Clinton. Moran went to Minnesota ten days later for first baseman Vic Power, a stylish defensive performer with a fine wit and sense of humor. Asked once about a ticket he had received for jaywalking, the Puerto Rican said: "You know, you have signs here for everything. Above the water fountain it says for whites only. In the restaurant it says for whites only. On the bus it says for whites only. So when the light turns green and I see all the whites crossing I assume that green light is for whites only and I wait for it to turn red so I can cross."

Power was Adcock's late inning caddy, coming on for defensive purposes.

Chance seldom needed a replacement. This was the one season it all came together for the talented farm boy, who was easily the game's best pitcher in 1964. He set club records for wins (20), ERA (1.65), shutouts (11), complete games (15), strikeouts in a game (15), strikeouts in a season (207), innings pitched (278⅓), consecutive scoreless innings (28) and consecutive shutouts (3). Five of his shutouts were by a 1–0 score, a major league record.

Chance went into the season angry that he had not received a raise from his 13-18 season in 1963, and it was his constant source of motivation, a carrot that Haney kept dangling in front of him and then withdrawing when Chance seemed certain to take a bite. He got the raise only after the 1964 season ended, only after he had become the youngest man ever to win the Cy Young.

His dominance was best illustrated by a 4-0 record and incredible 0.18 ERA against the powerful Yankees. On the few occasions when Chance needed relief, Rigney found a new stopper in Lee, an intimidating right-hander who stood 6-foot-3 and weighed 230 pounds when he was in shape.

The Angels drafted Lee for $25,000 from Batavia of the Pittsburgh system, where he had won 20 of 22 decisions, striking out 240 in 185 innings. Lee challenged hitters with the same vigor he challenged the curfew rules. He once drew a whopping fine when Haney discovered him romancing a young lady in the bullpen golf cart. He played hard and lived hard, and he expressed the opinion that his best years might have extended beyond the three he spent with the Angels if Rigney had not become a Captain Hook, burning out his arm by calling on him at the first sign of trouble.

Lee's 1964 emergence came at a time when the venerable Art Fowler had been assigned to pitch strictly batting practice. Lee responded with 17 saves before breaking his hand on September 5 when he hit an iron railing as he swung at a drunk, taunting fan near the bullpen in Boston's Fenway Park. He appeared in 64 games that year, 69 in 1965 and 61 in 1966, after which he was traded to the Dodgers for pitcher Nick Willhite.

The major trade of the winter of 1964 sent Belinsky to Philadelphia for pitcher Rudy May and first baseman Costen Shockley, who did not report until late in spring training because of a contract dispute with the Phillies. Shockley quit halfway through the 1965 season because he was unhappy being so far from his Delaware home, and also he felt he could earn more as a construction worker. May spent five seasons with the Angels, never quite realizing a potential he would later fulfill with Baltimore, Montreal and the New York Yankees.

Belinsky, familiar with Philadelphia because of his years in Trenton, said, "It's a hip town. They know what's happening. Whenever we were looking for fun we'd go to Philly."

Bo didn't have much fun this time, and he eventually added to the litany of things Philadelphia fans are willing to boo by claiming they'd even boo a funeral.

As Bo's career moved toward a premature death, the Angels were fortunate they didn't have to play their 1965 season in Philadelphia. It was their last season in Los Angeles and the lamest of their lame duck seasons. They were rained out of the season opener, lost to Cleveland, 7–1, while making three errors the next day and then had it turn worse.

Lee's 21 saves helped retain a measure of respectability, but Haney addressed the team in midseason and said, "We either get one hundred percent hustle or some of you won't go to Anaheim."

The tragic death of pitcher Dick Wantz in May left the team in a persistently somber mood. Ken McBride, the most consistent pitcher during those early years but the victim of a series of injuries during the 1964 and 1965 seasons, was sent to the minors in August and did not return.

Frustrated by the voids in his own farm system, Haney's youth movement took a strange turn. Pitcher Jack Sanford, 36, was purchased from the Giants and pitcher Jim Coates, 34, was obtained from Seattle. Cy Young Award winner Dean Chance went from 20-9 to 15-10. This time Chance said he wasn't motivated so much by the prospect of a raise but by his desire to avoid a cut.

The season's highlight may have been a beanball brawl with Boston, triggered by Chance. It was more than a customary waltz, and the Red Sox emerged saying they would ultimately "get" Chance, a vendetta they never achieved. Bob Rodgers was fined $100 for throwing the first punch and said it represented $50 a swing.

"Don't be upset," Piersall cautioned him. "If you had my reputation you would have gotten 10 days and $500."

The Angels formally announced on September 2 that henceforth they would be the California Angels. That night they played like the Los Angeles Angels, losing to New York, 8–1.

They were 46-34 during that final year at Dodger Stadium and an overall 170-153 for the four years there. While management eagerly anticipated the escape from the Dodgers' shadow and O'Malley's accountants, the hitters talked of getting to a park with fairer dimensions and the pitchers bemoaned the departure from the spacious Ravine.

Asked if it would be a more difficult transition for the players or manager, Rigney said, "It will definitely be more difficult for the players. I'll have to do only one thing differently and that's manage better."

Jim Fregosi, Rigney's leader among the players, said, "The important thing is that having our own park with our own fans will mean a great deal for team pride. There won't be 10,000 people in the stands listening to the Dodgers."

Chapter

X

THAT STRANGE youth movement initiated by the purchase of seniors Jack Sanford and Jim Coates continued as the Angels waited out their Anaheim debut. During the winter of 1966, Haney signed pitcher Lou Burdette, 39, and third baseman Frank Malzone, 35, as free agents, traded outfield prospect Dick Simpson to Baltimore for first baseman Norm Siebern, 32, and purchased catcher Ed Bailey, 34, from the Cubs.

It was an indictment of the Angels' farm system, and it was soon being written that the Angels would not play just one Oldtimers Game in Anaheim, they would play 162.

Haney responded by saying that the club had to get off to a good start in Anaheim, that they were shooting for a big year, and that the poise, polish and spirit of the new veterans might rub off on the young players.

"We must make a good showing," the general manager said, "and that constitutes a first-division finish. From the stands we looked dead last year. We have to recapture the spirit and attitude of three years ago.''

Haney referred to the third-place finish of 1962, which the Angels clung to as some sort of talisman, hoping to regenerate a magic that had long since faded.

Bill Rigney greeted his team in spring training and said, ''We may be beaten this year because the other club is better, but it will not be because we didn't go to bed at night. I will not allow this team to leave its desire on the golf course or in a bar.

''We displayed a consistent lack of initiative last year, and we can't play in Anaheim the way we closed out Dodger Stadium. Some of the players think this is a one-way street. We allowed them to be masters of their own fate. Now the twenty-four hours of each day will be done my way.''

If this was an attempt to inform the Angels that their country club was being converted into a concentration camp, the results were not evident. The Angels' first season in Anaheim was their sixth overall, and it was not much different from those that had come before. Some may have questioned the Angels' dedication and attitude, but it seemed more a matter of talent—the lack of it—as the Angels finished sixth, 18 games behind pennant winning Baltimore, with an 80-82 record.

The Angels went to work in Anaheim with only five players remaining from the 1961 expansion draft—Dean Chance, Fred Newman, Bob Rodgers, Jim Fregosi and Albie Pearson.

They also went to work in Anaheim with only 5 farm products among the 28 players on the opening-day roster—Jim McGlothlin, Tom Satriano, Paul Schaal, Ed Kirkpatrick and Rick Reichardt.

The Angels did get an unexpected bonus in 1966 when second baseman Bobby Knoop, the personification of ''good field, no hit,'' slugged 17 homers and drove in 72 runs, both career highs.

Knoop, drafted from Denver in 1963, joined with Fregosi to form the American League's best double-play combination and four times in his six years with the team was voted the Owners' Trophy by his teammates as the club's most valuable and inspirational player.

Some considered him the best second baseman they had ever seen.

"Every pitcher who gets a raise should give it to Knoop," the veteran Malzone said.

"He's the greatest I've ever seen," coach Del Rice said, "and I've seen Joe Gordon and Bill Mazeroski and Red Schoendienst."

Knoop enjoyed his finest all-around year in 1966, when the Angels made their formal debut at Anaheim Stadium on April 19, losing to Chicago, 3–1, before a crowd of 31,660.

The game was delayed in starting 25 minutes when a water main burst in downtown Anaheim, creating a traffic jam that extended into Azusa and Cucamonga. The visiting manager, Eddie Stanky, was also enraged when an electrician could not be located, forcing the White Sox to take batting practice in the dark, when a cluster of lights blew out.

"Twenty-four million for a park," Stanky roared, "and they won't spend three dollars to give us lights."

Stanky made headlines again later that year when he categorized the theatrical Rigney as a "TV manager" and said Kansas City's Alvin Dark "and myself are the game's only serious managers."

"Eddie never liked guys from California," Rigney said of his former Giant teammate, "but I don't really know what he means and I don't really care. I just consider the source."

The "TV manager" may have done one of his best jobs in 1966, keeping the Angels in first-division contention by pleading, pushing, cajoling and maneuvering. Eleven of Rigney's hitters batted under .250, and the team average was .232.

The offense was so offensive that when the Angels scored 12 runs in the eighth inning of a 16–9 victory over Boston, Rigney, confined to his hotel room because of the flu and watching on television, said, "We've gone months without scoring 12 runs."

It was seldom easy for Rigney. There was seldom a laugher, baseball's term for a rout. He was constantly dealing with players who had learned their fundamentals in other organizations, rejects who brought varying approaches to the game's various plays, fringe and utility players who couldn't be relied on to look for signs and couldn't be relied on to respond when they did.

A measure of the failure, futility and frustration encountered by Haney's five-year plan is that the retreads led his club in virtually every category in 1966.

Adcock was the batting (.273) and home run (18) leader, while Sanford was the pitching leader at 13-7. Pearson retired after injuring his back in April, Reichardt underwent kidney surgery in July, and Chance, suffering from his mysterious infection, slumped to 12-17.

The Angels, at least, had their own home now, and attendance almost tripled, soaring from 566,727 in 1965 to 1,400,321 in 1966, which did not include the 40,735 who watched an April 9 exhibition with the Giants. The Angels lost that first-ever game in Anaheim Stadium, 9–3, but came back to defeat the Giants, 6–5, the next day when Fregosi homered in the 10th, inspiring a crowd of 23,061.

Of the Big A (Anaheim Stadium), Rigney said, "The first chill I ever received in this game came when I walked into the Polo Grounds for the first time. I received another when I walked into this park."

Dean Chance watched batting practice the first day and said, "I thought they were hitting golf balls. We've got three guys who are a cinch to hit 30 homers each—Jim Fregosi, Jose Cardenal and Paul Schaal."

Cardenal hit 16 homers, Fregosi 13 and Schaal 5, the cozier dimensions of Anaheim Stadium being nullified somewhat by the heavy night air that moves in from the ocean during the first half of every season.

Rigney was criticized for his tendency to display a quick hook with starting pitchers, to burn out hot relievers, but he consistently seemed to draw more out of the Angels than they were capable of giving. His strategic moves were seldom questioned, and he was definitely a newspaperman's manager, providing stories on games that otherwise weren't worth more than a sentence.

He ripped players, managers and umpires. He exhibited emotion, sensitivity and humor. He worked hard to provide something other than a cliché. He enjoyed being with the writers socially.

He once called on them at a home they had rented in Palm Springs, stepping over the drunk and prone form of a scribe who had gotten no farther than the front door. The next day, standing in the middle of the diamond while supervising a workout, Rigney spotted the writer slowly making his way into the dugout and bellowed in a voice that echoed throughout the stadium, "Morning, Jack, did you vacuum your bed?"

The camaraderie between Rigney and the media was such that one morning the entire press corps arrived at the workout wearing uniform tops with the number 18½ on them, a half digit above Rigney's 18.

There is this story reflective of his gregarious nature, of his unquestioned love of the spotlight, no matter where or when: Rigney was seated with a writer at Toots Shor's bar in New York when an eavesdropper heard the bartender ask "Mr. Rigney" if he would like another drink. The eavesdropper, believing that the bartender had said Wrigley instead of Rigney and that he was sitting next to the owner of the Chicago Cubs, pardoned himself and said, "Mr. Wrigley, could you tell me please why you've never put lights in your park?"

Rigney carried off the charade perfectly, luxuriating in the opportunity to spend twenty minutes explaining why "we just don't believe in night baseball." The eavesdropper thanked "Wrigley" profusely and scurried to a phone to inform family and friends of his experience.

Rigney's own phone rang constantly. He received frequent job offers from other clubs, a measure of his appeal and ability. The most tempting came in September of that first season in Anaheim. Detroit general manager Jim Campbell received Haney's permission to speak with Rigney and then flew to Anaheim to meet personally with the Angels' manager.

Campbell offered a three-year contract at a total close to $200,000, a remarkable sum at that time. Rigney spent several days considering it, during which period the Angels offered a one-year extension at $65,000. Rigney ultimately called Campbell and said he still had a job to finish with the Angels and that California was his home.

The Angels announced that Rigney would be back in 1967 but that his coaches—Del Rice, Jack Paepke, Marv Grissom and Salty Parker—would not be rehired, scapegoats for the string of sad summers, temporarily snapped in 1967 when the Angels played a significant role in one of the American League's most exciting pennant races ever, after mounting their own pennant challenge in midsummer.

Bob Lemon, Billy Herman, Mike Roarke and Don Heffner joined Rigney's coaching staff. General manager Haney then visited the trading market, where he found spirited interest in Dean Chance, whose deteriorating performance and inconsistent behavior in 1966 prompted the Angels, seeking hitting help, to make him expendable.

The best offer came from Minnesota, and on December 2 the Angels traded their Cy Young Award winner of 1964 for first baseman Don Mincher, outfielder Jimmie Hall and pitcher Pete Cimino.

"I'm not sure we'll ever find another arm like Dean's," Rigney said, "but we had to do something about our first base situation and overall hitting."

"I'm not surprised to be traded," Chance said, "but I am shocked that the Angels would trade me to an American League club. I'm shocked that they'd run the risk of letting me come back to haunt them."

Chance did come back, winning 20 games in 1967 and 16 in 1968, after which he injured his arm and was never again the same talent.

Hall and Cimino never fulfilled their promise, but Mincher led the club with 25 homers and 78 RBI in 1967 before succumbing to the jinx. He was beaned during the opening week of the 1968 season, his last with the Angels, and retired at the end of the 1970 season at 32.

The Angels headed for spring training in 1967 without Chance, without Belinsky, without 26 of the 30 players they had selected in the expansion draft. Rigney believed it was "the best club we've ever had. This is the first time I've ever felt this good about our prospects. This is the best eight we've ever had."

The opening-day lineup read: Paul Schaal, 3B; Jim Fregosi, SS; Rick Reichardt, LF; Don Mincher, 1B; Jimmie Hall, RF; José Cardenal, CF; Bob Rodgers, C; Bobby Knoop, 2B, and George Brunet, P.

The Angels beat Detroit's Denny McLain, 4–2, that day, Anaheim's ceremonial first pitch having been thrown by a right-hander named Ronald Reagan, and the optimistic glow became that much brighter on April 24 when a doubleheader sweep of Cleveland put the Angels in sole possession of first place for the first time since that memorable July 4, 1962.

The clubhouse celebration made it seem as if this was September 24 instead of April 24, and what followed was almost predictable. The Angels lost their next three games and then lost six in a row in mid-May. They were eight games under .500 on May 23 when Haney said, "It looks like we're dead. I haven't seen the spirit to battle back."

Unwilling to let what was expected to be their best season get away, Haney and Robert Reynolds held a unique clubhouse meeting with the team on May 24, Haney impersonating a football coach delivering his halftime oratory.

"Rig has talked his heart out," Haney told the press. "Maybe it will have some new meaning if it comes from someone else."

Rigney wasn't happy about the front office intervention. He said the clubhouse was his, the executive wing theirs.

"I believe the morale is good, damn good," he said heatedly.

There was no immediate improvement. The Angels were still eight games under .500 on June 2 when Reynolds said, "It's too early to make radical changes, but it's a blessing that Gene Autry has been in Japan and hasn't been here to see the way the team has played."

Three days later, Rigney, Haney and Reynolds held a summit meeting, after which Haney repeated his 1964 vow, saying Rigney would be "the manager for as long as I'm the general manager."

The Angels now finally began to move, winning five in a row, then 18 of 24 to reach .500 on July 1. They were now only seven games out of the lead, and Rigney, his confidence restored, was again saying he had a pennant contender.

The impetus was provided by a stable pitching staff that lacked the big winner but got 12 wins for the season from both McGlothlin, who set a club record in midsummer with 33 consecutive scoreless innings, and Minnie Rojas, the Cuban right-hander, who set a club record for appearances (72) and saves (22). Rojas, paralyzed in the tragic car accident that followed the 1968 season, had the best ERA (2.51) among the regular pitchers on a staff that led the league in ERA (3.19).

The Angels were 4½ out and 5 games over .500 on July 10 and within 1½ games on August 14 when the first five teams were separated by only 2½ games.

The league-leading Minnesota Twins moved into Anaheim for a three-game series on that day, and it was the beginning of the week that was for the Angels, the week that destroyed their pennant aspirations.

A throwing error by Fregosi and two RBI by an unlikely hero, reserve shortstop Jackie Hernandez, a throw-in in the deal that sent Chance to Minnesota, gave the Twins a 2–1 victory in the opener of the series and seemed to strip the Angels of their heart.

Jim Perry shut them out, 4–0, and Dean Chance beat them, 5–1, sending the Angels limping to Boston, where they lost four straight games, emerging 6½ games behind the Twins, a stunning and sudden disparity that proved insurmountable.

The Boston series was the one in which Tony Conigliaro, one of the game's best young players, a hitter of unlimited potential, suffered his almost fatal beaning when a fast ball thrown by Jack Hamilton, a pitcher who made his living with the spitball but who in this case insisted he had not put saliva on the ball—an assertion supported by catcher Rodgers and most of the Red Sox—struck Conigliaro on the left side of his face, catching both bone and batting helmet.

Those who were there in Fenway Park and heard that sound will never forget it.

The pitcher and batter were never the same.

Hamilton, a journeyman right-hander who had been obtained from the Mets in a June trade that sent Nick Willhite to New York, seemed haunted by the incident and was out of baseball within two years.

Conigliaro, 22 at the time, a strikingly handsome Italian who had hit 104 homers in his first three and a half seasons with the Red Sox, lost significant vision in his left eye, sat out the 1968 season, came back to hit 20 homers for the Red Sox in 1969 and 36 in 1970, but then suffered additional deterioration in his sight and retired abruptly in midseason of 1971, having been traded, ironically, to the Angels during the previous winter.

The Conigliaro beaning took place on a Friday night in the first game of a trip that remains one of the Angels' most memorable ever. Boston won the next day's "pitchers' duel," 12–11, and then swept a doubleheader on Sunday, the Angels blowing an 8–0 lead in the second game, highlighted by a verbal and physical exchange between umpire Bill Valentine and Boston manager Dick Williams, a vigorous encounter in which almost the entire Boston team was called on to restrain Williams.

The Angels then moved on to Cleveland where Jim Coates and Tony Horton exchanged punches during a 6–4 Angels win; Luis Tiant struck out 16 in pitching a 3–2 Cleveland win; the Angels got 25 hits in a 16–5 romp; and Sam McDowell struck out 10 Angels in a 3–2 Cleveland win.

The club headed for Baltimore, where a Friday night doubleheader was rained out, the second game of a Saturday night doubleheader was rained out after Mincher had won the opener with a three-run homer in the ninth, and the Sunday doubleheader was also rained out.

The Angels continued to play aggressively, but were unable to improve on their fifth-place standing. They did, however, turn the Great Race in favor of Boston by winning two of three from Minnesota (beating Chance in the final game of the series) and two of four from Detroit during the final week of a season in which the top three clubs were separated by only 1½ games entering the final day.

A six-run rally—ignited by Fregosi's single and capped by Fregosi's two-run single—in the eighth inning of the second game of a doubleheader with Detroit on the season's next-to-last day had wiped out a 4–2 Detroit lead and the prospect of a sweep, leaving the Tigers in a position where they had to beat the Angels on the last day in a doubleheader to gain a tie with either Boston or Minnesota, who were playing at Fenway Park.

The Tigers won the opener 6–4 as Boston beat Chance and Minnesota, but in the emotional nightcap, in the lingering twilight of a cold and gray afternoon at Tiger Stadium, Rick Reichardt and Don Mincher hit clutch home runs and George Brunet came out of the bullpen in the ninth inning, for only the third time in 40 appearances, and got Dick McAuliffe, who had grounded into only one double play all year, to ground into another with two on and one out, preserving an 8–5 Angels victory that gave the pennant to Boston.

The Angels finished 5½ back with an 84-77 record.

Johnny Podres, the former Dodger star who was wrapping up his career in Detroit, sat in the silent Tigers clubhouse and said, "If the Angels had played like this all season there wouldn't have been a great race. The Angels would have won it easily."

Rigney concurred, but said that his team's play during the final week had provided a foundation for 1968.

"We learned what it takes to win the pennant," he said. "We learned the meaning of guts and what you have to stand up to emotionally. What we learned we won't forget. They'll never forget what they went through that final week."

So much for long memories. The 1968 season was one of the Angels' most disappointing. The Angels went from 84–77 to 67–95, finishing eighth, 36 games behind the Tigers, who finally achieved the goal they came so close to achieving the year before.

It all went bad for the Angels, who could have guessed as much on opening day when they lost in New York, 1–0, and then had to flee a burning plane at La Guardia Airport just after taking their seats.

Mincher was beaned by Sam McDowell a few days later and appeared in just 120 games, hitting just 13 homers. Third baseman Paul Schaal was beaned by Boston's José Santiago in June and appeared in just 60 games, batting just .210.

Minnie Rojas, suffering from a sore arm, the result perhaps of his 72 appearances in 1967, appeared in just 38 games, saving but 5, which was 17 fewer than the previous year.

Rick Reichardt hit 21 homers and drove in 73 runs, but the team batting average was a league low .227.

George Brunet was the leading pitcher with an unattractive 13-17.

The Angels heard Gene Autry deliver a rare clubhouse pep talk on August 30, but Autry should have saved his voice for another recording. The Angels finished the year with a 32-49 record in Anaheim, losing 7 of their last 8 games.

Marvin Milkes, Haney's important right arm, left to become general manager in Seattle, while Cedric Tallis, the most important cog in the move to Anaheim, left to become general manager of Kansas City's expansion team.

Rigney would have left, too, since he received managerial offers from the Giants, Twins, White Sox and Royals, but Autry's offer of a two-year contract influenced him to stay. It was a vote of confidence for the manager that would not be repeated ten months later.

Chapter
XI

THE FUTURE of Bill Rigney was not the only subject discussed in the boardroom of Golden West Broadcasters during the 1968 season.

The Signal Companies, a Los Angeles conglomerate, approached Gene Autry with a deal that allowed GWB's minority shareholders to sell out while Autry retained majority control. Signal ultimately acquired 49.9% for $25 million. The arrangement also gave Signal first option on obtaining Autry's 50.1% for $20 million at the time of his death.

Leonard Firestone, who owned 30% of the Angels in 1968, objected to Signal's corporate invasion of a sports franchise —a franchise already owned by a corporation—and offered his stock to Autry and the other shareholders, who bought him out for $9 million. The club's ownership structure did not change again until 1974, when all of the minority shareholders —most having reached an age when they were thinking of estate planning—agreed to sell their stock to Golden West Broadcasting. Robert Reynolds, Autry's longtime partner and the club president since the start, received $7.5 million, leaving Autry and Signal the only shareholders.

The boardroom decision that had the more significant impact on the club's operation was reached in September of 1968 and involved Fred Haney, who had turned 70 in April of that year.

Frustrated by the inability of the Angels to manufacture a series of solid seasons and believing the farm and scouting systems had not produced in the anticipated manner, Autry and Reynolds decided it was time for a younger man to carry on, for close friend Haney to step down.

They met with Haney and told him they still retained confidence in him but they believed age had become an issue. They offered him a position as club consultant at his same salary.

Haney was disappointed. He knew that the consultant's position translated to a title without substance, and he tried to talk Autry and Reynolds out of their decision while not saying anything that would impair their long relationship or sound ungrateful for their years of support.

"Fred knew that Gene and Bob were under pressure to make a change," Haney's widow, Florence, said years later, "but Fred wouldn't think of saying anything that would hurt anyone. He would have done anything in the world for Gene and Bob."

Haney agreed to become consultant to a general manager not yet selected. The three candidates were Giants general manager Chub Feeney, Mets general manager Bob Sheffing and former Dodgers vice president Dick Walsh, then in the third year of a five-year contract as commissioner of the North American Soccer League.

Both Feeney and Scheffing demanded stock arrangements that the Angels were unwilling to meet, leaving Walsh the primary candidate. It seemed an improbable alliance, since the Angels and Walsh had argued frequently during the four years in which the Angels were tenants at Dodger Stadium, where Walsh, Walter O'Malley's vice president in charge of saying no, had served as director of stadium operations.

In that time, Reynolds said later, the Angels developed admiration and respect for Walsh's knowledge and energy, for his unyielding, uncompromising and no-nonsense approach, traits soon described in a far less flattering manner.

Golden West executives Bert West and Stan Spero were dispatched to New York to sound out Walsh, who responded with enthusiasm to the proposal that eventually took the form of a seven-year contract, the announcement being made on September 23, 1968, the same day it was announced that Rigney had been rehired for two years.

"I look upon this as the start of a new era for the Angels," Reynolds said. "I'm confident that under Dick Walsh and Bill Rigney our team will attain the capabilities that we still believe it possesses."

Rigney was fired eight months later. Walsh was fired with four years remaining on his contract. The new era became the most tumultuous in Angels history, the capabilities disintegrating under a cloud of controversy.

How it happened is more easily explained than why. Richard Bishop Walsh, Jr., was a man of unquestioned ability and intelligence. He emerged from the reputation-shattering experience with the Angels to resume his schooling, received a law degree and ultimately became director of the Los Angeles Convention Center.

He had previously been an All-City third baseman at Los Angeles High School, his desire to play professionally frustrated by World War II. He was 17 when he received an officer's commission and 18 when he became an infantry platoon leader in the Pacific conflict with Japan. He was hired by the Dodgers when the war ended and assigned to learn the business literally from the ground up, sweeping out stadiums, punching tickets, selling advertising.

He had been with the Dodgers for 18 years when he accepted the offer from the North American Soccer League, reasoning he had gone as far as he could with the Dodgers since there were two heirs on the horizon, Peter Bavasi, son of the general manager, and Peter O'Malley, son of the owner.

"I'm returning to my first love," Walsh said at the time of his hiring by the Angels, a statement some soon questioned, appalled that anyone would treat their love with Walsh's callousness.

The belief that Walsh would supply a direction and discipline previously absent soon gave way to the realization that Walsh's discipline represented dictatorship and his direction was leading directly to doom.

His relationship with the city of Anaheim dissolved in the same manner as his relationship with the players and front office associates. City officials accused him of lies and broken promises. A former club executive said, "He was always trying to set traps and catch you in lies. He was always using his own lies to set the traps."

Traveling secretary Tommie Ferguson left to become vice president of the Milwaukee Brewers. Farm and scouting director Roland Hemond left to become vice president of the Chicago White Sox. Speakers Bureau director Johnny Lindell left to become security director at Santa Anita racetrack.

Ferguson recalled the day close friend Rigney was fired. "Walsh sent me to his hotel room with the airline ticket for Rig's flight home," Ferguson said. "When I got back to the stadium, Walsh asked me if I had brought the club suitcase Rig had been using."

Stunned by Walsh's cold pettiness, Ferguson said, "No, I'll leave that up to you."

Walsh had a hand in every department. He was accused of failing to delegate authority.

"There was no organization when I arrived," he said. "I had to build one. I made sure I was in the middle of every department at first. Once we had a format, I stayed clear. I had regular staff meetings and I even had meetings just for the secretaries. I felt they had a right to know what was going on."

Of the conflicts with the city, Walsh said, "We were being charged indiscriminately, such as the salary for a maintenance man on a twelve-month basis rather than simply the duration of the baseball season. That's minutia, perhaps, but it added up."

Little things seemed to eat at Walsh. He sent a letter to the equipment man saying the players had been using too many towels. The players responded with a sign that read: "2 Towels for Regulars and 1 for Extra Men. Pitchers Who Are Not Used Must Shower at Home."

The players believed Walsh was attempting to use fear as a

motivation. One pitcher was sued for divorce when his wife got hold of a letter Walsh sent him in which he said the pitcher would not receive a raise because he had contracted a venereal disease. Personalities meant nothing. It was all statistics.

"I don't want to get close to the players because I don't want to lose my objectivity," Walsh said. "The players aren't entertained in my house and I'm not entertained in theirs."

Walsh's dispassion was seen in 1971. Six-time All-Star Jim Fregosi, the club leader, a man to whom Walsh had just given a three-year contract, which was designed, he said, to eventually help Fregosi become the Angels' manager, developed a tumor on his foot. Walsh, with several other players hurt and his team in tatters, refused to let Fregosi undergo the required operation. It was not until midseason, when Fregosi checked himself into the hospital, that the shortstop left the lineup.

The players' distaste for the man they called the "Smiling Python" manifested itself in 1971 when, spotting Walsh standing in foul territory down the left field line during batting practice, they moved up in the batting cage and purposely tried to hit line drives in the direction of Walsh's back. Manager Harold (Lefty) Phillips soon caught on and cancelled the rest of batting practice, sending the players to the clubhouse in the manner of misbehaving youngsters.

It was in 1971 that the A in Big A came to stand for "Agony." It all fell apart and manager Phillips said, "I'm afraid there's going to be real violence in the clubhouse. Somebody is going to hit somebody else over the head with a stool . . . or worse."

The "worse" referred to the guns and knives that many of the players began to carry as the symptoms of disintegration became acute. The clubhouse became a place where Angels feared to tread. There were fights, arguments and a continuous process of internal decay, much of it stemming from Alex Johnson, the talented but temperamental outfielder who seemed to carry a deep-seated hatred for all humanity.

Johnson had been acquired in one of a series of trades that left Hemond shaking his head and saying it was "chaotic." Walsh said he didn't really believe in building a team through trade but that there was no time for a five-year plan, that you have to go for broke when competing with the Dodgers and that there wasn't anything in the Angels' farm system when he took over.

Those who watched Walsh, a man with little experience in the area of personnel, do his wheeling and dealing could have sworn he was using farm talent to put across his trades.

Aurelio Rodriguez, a brilliant third baseman fresh out of the farm system, was coupled with Rick Reichardt and traded to Washington in 1970 for Ken McMullen. This wasn't entirely Walsh's doing, since he was prodded by Phillips, who found it difficult communicating with the Spanish-speaking Rodriguez, still a major leaguer a decade later.

Phillips' forte was execution, not elocution. He once said, "Our phenoms ain't phenomenating." Another gem was "It's all water under the dam." Phillips had a tough time communicating with everyone, no matter what language they spoke.

Pedro Borbon, who spoke mostly Spanish and threw mostly fast balls during a distinguished career as a big league relief pitcher, was lifted out of the farm system and packaged with Jim McGlothlin and Vern Geishert in the 1969 trade by which Walsh acquired Alex Johnson, who had already created a legacy of problems in Philadelphia, St. Louis and Cincinnati.

A year later, pitching prospect Greg Garrett went to Cincinnati for pitcher Jim Maloney, who never won a game for the Angels. Outfielder Bill Voss went to Milwaukee for pitcher Gene Brabender, who was optioned to the minors even before the season began.

Pitching prospect Tom Bradley was coupled with Tom Egan and maturing outfielder Jay Johnstone in a trade with the White Sox that brought Ken Barry, who batted .221 with the Angels, seldom used infielder Syd O'Brien, and pitcher Billy Wynne, optioned before the season began.

Second baseman Doug Griffin joined outfielder Jarvis Tatum and relief pitcher Ken Tatum in a package exchanged for Boston catcher Jerry Moses (a third-stringer with the Angels), pitcher Ray Jarvis (optioned before the season's start) and the star-crossed Tony Conigliaro, obviously made expendable by the Red Sox for the simple reason that his sight had begun to deteriorate again.

These trades were all in the future when the Angels gathered in the "Carrot Capital" of Holtville for spring training in 1969.

Rigney and Walsh were anxious to expiate the eighth-place finish of the season before, and Rigney knew he was not really the new general manager's man. That, of course, was Phillips, hired initially as director of player personnel and then assigned to Rigney's staff as pitching coach, a move that surprised Rigney but which he did not entirely object to, since he respected Phillips' knowledge of the game. Rigney had asked Phillips, a pitching coach under the Dodgers' Walter Alston, to assist him on a part-time basis during spring training, and Walsh responded by putting Phillips in uniform on a full-time basis, wasting no time in getting one of his own people in the clubhouse.

The pressure on Rigney was evident from the first day of spring training when, after chatting with the press prior to the initial workout, Rigney walked away and Walsh said, "That gray-haired gentleman has only a two-year contract and I have a seven-year contract."

The American and National leagues split into Eastern and Western divisions in 1969, and that was the reason the Angels didn't finish eighth again. They finished third in the West, 13 games behind Minnesota, with a 71-91 record.

The Angels' team batting average of .230 was last in the league, and they were also last in home runs, RBI, runs scored, hits and total bases. Johnstone led the club with a .270 batting average, but he could not prevent the Angels from being shut out 19 times, a league high.

Andy Messersmith, the best pitcher ever developed by the Angels' system, was 16-11, but his 0-5 start contributed to Rigney's firing, as did the absence of a relief pitcher. Rigney kept asking for Ken Tatum, the right-handed relief pitcher then at Hawaii, but Walsh did not respond until after Phillips had taken over. Tatum helped Phillips attain a team record of 60 wins-63 losses with 22 saves, a 7-2 record and an ERA of 1.36.

The inevitable began to close in on Rigney with the first pitch of the new season. The Angels stranded 10 runners and lost to the new expansion team from Seattle, 4–3.

"Again," Rigney said in frustration, "we didn't do the things we talked about all spring. Twice we had runners on third base and didn't score them simply by making the right type of out.''

A 15–1 loss on May 5 to the expansion team from Kansas City prompted Walsh to say, "When we fall behind we just go through the motions. This is a unique experience for me and I don't like it.''

"At least," Rigney said, "no one got hurt.''

Two weeks later, Walsh again talked about the "defeatist attitude" and traded the most respected and best liked Angel, second baseman Bobby Knoop, to Chicago for second baseman Sandy Alomar.

Knoop's former teammates reacted angrily to the trade, but it may have been one of Walsh's best, since Alomar, 26, was five years younger than Knoop and had more offensive weapons, including speed. He stole 20 of the Angels' 54 bases that year and 35 in 1970. He had 22 game-winning hits in 1970 and extended what would become a club record for consecutive games played, a streak that reached 648 before Alomar broke his leg in 1973.

The deal for the "Iron Pony," a play by Alomar's teammates on Lou Gehrig's nickname of the Iron Horse, was consummated on the day that the Angels left on the trip that led squarely to Rigney's firing.

There had been the 8-18 death march of 1961 and a 1-8 excursion in 1967, but there had never been an exercise in futility to match the 0-10 trip which ended with Fregosi, aware that Rigney's firing had to be imminent, saying the manager wasn't to blame. Fregosi's plea was too late.

Walsh had already called Autry and Reynolds to tell them, "Rig has lost control of the team. I don't feel we can win. I don't think we can turn it around with him in there.''

Reynolds received Walsh's call while on a vacation in India. He reacted by sending his wife to visit the Taj Mahal with friends while he paced the room for two days, trying to digest what Walsh had told him.

Autry was on a business trip to New York when Walsh called. "Perhaps I knew it was inevitable," Autry said in reflection, "but it was still a blow. I told Dick that Rig was not only the only manager we had ever known, he was our friend.

I told him that if he was convinced a change had to be made, then let's do it at once since there's no sense in waiting. I asked him who he had in mind."

Walsh's answer was Lefty Phillips. Autry would concede years later that it was at this juncture he made a serious mistake by not insisting Walsh elevate Chuck Tanner, a communicative fireball who would later lead Pittsburgh to a World Championship. Tanner was then managing the Angels' Hawaii farm club, having been in the system as player and manager almost from the start, a man totally familiar with the players then on the Angels' roster.

"I suppose," Autry said, looking back, "there are three kinds of owners. One is the type who puts up the money and runs the club himself, serving as his own general manager. The second is the type who hires a professional to run the club, then stays out of the way and keeps score. The third is the type who keeps such a low profile that the players and fans hardly know he exists.

"I like to think I belong to the second category. I have tried hard not to interfere with the men on the firing line. I am consulted on major decisions and the final approval is mine, but I don't recall ever overruling someone who felt strongly his way was right. I have made an effort to know the players. I drop by the clubhouse from time to time, and I try to write personal notes to each player who is traded away after long service with the club. I have never had any desire to go on the field or be in the dugout. I have wondered often why a manager did this or that, but I have always tried to restrain my second-guessing. I have never ordered a manager to play a certain player, and I have never called a manager at three in the morning to ask why he didn't play the infield back with one out.

"Lefty Phillips was a fine man with a solid reputation as coach and scout, but he was a disaster as manager and I will accept the blame for not insisting Tanner be hired. I will also accept the blame for not dealing promptly with the Alex Johnson situation, but again I thought we had professionals running the show."

Rigney was fired on May 26, 1969, Autry announcing that "We simply don't believe the Angels are a last-place team."

Almost every reporter who had covered the club during its eight-plus years went to Rigney's Anaheim hotel room to share a drink with him following the announcement. There was no anger or bitterness on Rigney's part. He had a contract that entitled him to be paid for three more years, and he would soon be in a situation that would allow him to enjoy a last laugh of sorts.

"Sometimes a change in managers is what it takes," Rigney acknowledged as he packed the suitcase that would ultimately be returned to Walsh. "It gives the players a reason for why they have been bad. The saddest thing about this is that, in the eight years, the organization really didn't improve any."

Said the Smiling Python, "I said this spring that we are capable of contending and I still believe that. I had to move now or forgo the entire season. The club was down and beating itself too often. It was waiting for lightning to strike. It was waiting to be beaten."

With a .216 team batting average and 4.10 ERA at the time of Rigney's firing, it seldom had to wait long.

Phillips understood the scapegoat implications of Rigney's dismissal. "He was a very sound manager," the new manager said. "I'd say that 95% of the time I agreed with the way he did things. The other 5% you could go either way."

In another time and place, Harold Phillips may not have been the disaster Autry perceived. He was a slow-moving, slope-shouldered, pot-bellied man of whom Johnny Podres, the Dodgers' pitching star, once said, "No one looks worse in a uniform nor knows as much about baseball." A student of pitching and fundamentals, and a man credited with signing many of the Dodgers' top players of the 1960s, Phillips knew and cared little about syntax, or about the players' alleged need for communication. He made his points in brief bursts of shattered English, waving an unlit cigar, a chaw of tobacco dirtying his uniform and making it that much more difficult to understand what he was saying. The cigar was never lit because Phillips was an asthmatic. He was only 53, in fact, when he died suddenly of an asthma attack on June 12, 1972, having been fired with Walsh during the previous winter.

The story is told with compassion of the night in 1969 when pitcher Phil Ortega, a Yaqui Indian who couldn't handle his firewater, appeared in the lobby of the Muehlbach Hotel in Kansas City wearing only underwear. The call went to manager Phillips, who piled out of bed and boarded an elevator, failing to notice that every floor had been punched. By the time an angry and excited Phillips had reached the lobby, he was wheezing so badly that he could barely walk or talk. He found Ortega, however, and had no trouble making the pitcher understand he had just been fined $1,000.

In another time and place, without the distractions created by an Ortega, an Alex Johnson, a Tony Conigliaro, Phillips might have been able to put his knowledge to work. He might have been able to do it with the Angels except that he received virtually no support from Dick Walsh, his friend. Phillips became the fall guy, hearing only sounds of silence from Walsh, Autry and Reynolds. The good friends Phillips and Walsh seldom even talked during their final days with the Angels.

The man who pushed both over the brink, who did even more, perhaps, to tear the organization apart than the man who traded for him, was Alex Johnson. He was acquired from Cincinnati in November of 1969, the Angels also getting utility infielder Chico Ruiz and seldom-used pitcher Mel Queen in the same deal.

Walsh, either through naivete or total disregard for Johnson's track record for disruptions, said, "I'm elated. Alex will answer many of our problems."

And, in some measure, Alex did, at least in 1970. He became the first Angel ever to collect 200 hits in a season, two coming on the final night when he went 2 for 3 to finish with a .329 batting average, edging Boston's Carl Yastrzemski for the league title by .003.

Johnson was the catalyst, as a team that had the league's lowest batting average in 1969 set club records for hits (1,391) and average (.251) in 1970. Jim Fregosi, batting ahead of Johnson, had 16 game-winning hits, 22 homers, 82 RBI and a .278 average. Jim Spencer, batting behind Johnson, hit .274.

Rib and shoulder injuries diluted Messersmith's effectiveness between May and August, but left-hander Clyde Wright, a farm system product out of Carson-Newman College in Jefferson City, Tennessee, went from 2 wins in 1969 to a club record 22 in 1970, including a no-hitter against Oakland, the

Angels' first no-hitter since Belinsky's in 1962. Another promising pitcher, Tom Murphy, won 16 games while Tatum saved 17, though after he beaned Paul Blair of Baltimore at Anaheim Stadium in August, Tatum was never again the same pitcher. The hard-throwing right-hander, a man who saved 39 games in his first two seasons, became reluctant to throw his best fast ball inside, and this was a key reason for his inclusion in the trade for Conigliaro.

The Angels were only three back of Minnesota on September 4 when the Twins, managed then by a man named Rigney, initiated a three-game sweep of California, plunging the Angels into a nine-game losing streak during which Phillips said:

"I watch us play now and I feel like patting myself on the back. I must have been a mastermind for three-fourths of the season."

Phillips also said, "We finished 26 games out last year and it would mean quite a bit to the franchise as well as to each man if we could finish second. However, from what I've seen, I've got some players who are too dumb to realize it. There is a definite lack of maturity."

The Angels frustrated Phillips by tailing off to finish third, 12 games behind Rigney's pennant-winning Twins. The 86-76 record was 15 games better than in 1969, and attendance spiraled from an Anaheim low of 758,388 to 1,077,741. Walsh and Phillips had reason to believe they were doing a few things right—though not enough reason, perhaps, to disregard the time bomb that was Alex Johnson. Johnson at times in 1970 had angered his manager and teammates with an inexplicable lack of hustle, had strained nerves with his taunting of teammates and writers, had displayed the temperament that had made him a liability in Cincinnati, St. Louis and Philadelphia.

Alex Johnson had it all—strength, speed, instincts—but it was impossible to quell the fires that raged within him. A Prince Charming away from the park, his behavior when he put on the uniform once prompted his wife to apologize to the wives of the other Angel players.

In one of his few coherent interviews, one of his few interviews of *any* kind, Johnson said his attitude was a response to racial injustice.

"Hell, yes, I'm bitter," he said. "I've been bitter since I

learned I was black. The society into which I was born and in which I grew up and in which I play ball today is anti-black. My attitude is nothing more than a reaction to their attitude. But they [the whites] don't keep their hatreds to themselves. They go out of their way to set up barriers, to make dirty little slights so that you're aware of their messed-up feelings.''

Johnson never tried to hide his own. He and Ruiz exchanged punches by the batting cage in September of 1970, and there were constant confrontations with the media. He poured coffee grounds into the typewriter of the *Los Angeles Herald Examiner*'s Dick Miller, and he daily delivered obscenity-laced tirades that made it impossible for the writers to interview Johnson or anyone else in the Angels' clubhouse. The club's press corps ultimately filed a formal complaint with the league office, prompting the Angels' publicist, George Lederer, on behalf of Johnson, to send each writer a telegram in which Johnson said, ''. . . in the future I will not talk with you in any manner, offensive or otherwise.''

The 1970 season was a mere prelude to the nightmare of 1971, when Johnson's antics were compounded by the players' mounting unhappiness with Walsh, by the front office's belief that the trades for Berry, Conigliaro and Maloney had ensured a pennant, and by the performance of Conigliaro, who settled into a Newport Beach apartment next door to actress Raquel Welch.

If that alone was not enough to create envy among his Angels, Conigliaro soon began to experience a nagging string of little injuries, creating a feeling among his teammates that he was malingering. Conigliaro returned from one hospital trip and found a stretcher in front of his locker with his uniform laid out on it, a pair of crutches tied together as a coat of arms, and the whole thing splashed with catsup for blood.

''If Conigliaro does for us what he did for Boston,'' Walsh had said at the time of the trade, ''then I can't help but think in terms of a pennant.''

What Conigliaro had done for Boston in the second year of his comeback from the near-fatal beaning of 1967 was hit 36 home runs and drive in 116 runs. What he did for the Angels in 1971 was hit 4 home runs and drive in 15 runs. He appeared in only 74 games before the new deterioration in his left eye prompted him to hold a 5 A.M. press conference on July 10, announcing his retirement. The unusual hour stemmed from the fact that the Angels had gone past midnight before losing a 1–0, 20-inning decision to Oakland. Conigliaro had been unable to sleep because of his hitless effort and two run-ins with umpire Merle Anthony. The weight of the season and the uncertainty with his vision prompted him to summon the writers at a time when they are generally comatose.

"This is something I had to do," he said, referring to his retirement, "or I'd end up in a straitjacket with the other nuts.

"I almost lost my mind out there tonight. I was doing things on the field and saying things on the bench that I didn't know I was saying or doing.

"I was saying good-by to baseball."

Manager Phillips responded by saying Conigliaro belonged in an institution. The Angels placed him on the voluntary retired list instead and terminated his salary. Conigliaro later filed a grievance through the Major League Players Association seeking his second-half salary. He argued that the Angels should have been aware of his eye problem and placed him on the disabled list before he reached a mental state that led him to retire. An arbitrator ruled in favor of Conigliaro, and the Angels were forced to pay him an additional $40,000.

The decision was reached after Walsh had been fired and he said, "There was not much I could have done differently in the Conigliaro situation. Boston had guaranteed that he was physically sound, that there was no problem with his eye. If I had remained as general manager I'd have demanded compensation from the Red Sox."

Conigliaro's retirement came about two weeks after the Angels had finally suspended Johnson, who drew 29 fines totaling $3,000 through the season's first 71 games.

Phillips' problems with Johnson had flared again in spring training of 1971 when the batting champion stood in the shade of a light tower while on defense during an exhibition game and was then benched when he failed to run out a ground ball in the eighth inning. He was benched again the next day when he again failed to run out a ground ball, establishing a pattern that haunted and hounded the Angels for the next five months. Johnson was in and out of the lineup, in and out of the doghouse. The lingering crises undermined morale, cost Phillips what respect he had with the team and created a cleavage between Phillips and Walsh as they disagreed over who should have done what and when with Johnson.

Remarkably, the outfielder viewed it all as some sort of conspiracy and said he would rather be playing in hell than Anaheim. There were those who insisted that Anaheim had become just that.

"I'm not writing about baseball," complained one reporter. "I'm writing about World War III."

Walsh could have initiated an armistice simply by supporting his manager on any of the numerous occasions when Phillips told the team that Johnson "will never again play for the Angels."

But that kind of support never came—until it was really too late. The taunts, the lack of hustle, led the Angels to take things into their own hands. An enraged Ken Berry charged at Johnson in the clubhouse, forcing teammates to intervene, knowing neither Berry, nor anyone else really, was a match for the muscular Johnson.

Clyde Wright threateningly raised a clubhouse stool after Johnson had thrown a Coke at him, prompting Johnson to say, "Go ahead. You get one swing with the stool. Then you're mine."

Wright backed off.

Ultimately, however, Chico Ruiz, one of several armed Angels and a favorite target for Johnson's obscene diatribes, allegedly pulled a gun on his tormentor during a clubhouse dispute, and it was a few days later, on June 26, 1971, that the Angels finally suspended Johnson for "failure to hustle and improper mental attitude."

Johnson responded with a grievance filed through the Players Association. Executive director Marvin Miller argued that Johnson had been seeing a psychiatrist for emotional stress and should have been placed on the disabled list. The arbitrator agreed, ruling in September that the Angels had to put Johnson back on their roster and provide him with his salary. Johnson was back, but not for long.

The Angels began their postseason housecleaning by trading Johnson and catcher Moses, unhappy over his lack of playing time ("He ain't exactly Gabby Hartnett," Phillips said at one point), to Cleveland for outfielder Vada Pinson, infielder-outfielder Frank Baker and pitcher Alan Foster.

Only Pinson made a significant contribution in 1972, but this was a trade that represented addition via subtraction. Johnson's departure eradicated a malignancy, removing the man who had stripped the Angels of any chance of living up to their preseason role of favorite in the American League West.

The Angels had won their first seven games in 1971 and were then heard from again only because of their clubhouse chaos. Andy Messersmith won 20 games and Clyde Wright 16, but with Johnson (who batted just .259), Conigliaro and Fregosi frequently out of the lineup, the team batting average fell to .231.

The Angels finished fourth with a 76-86 record, 25½ games behind Oakland after playing at a 44-43 pace following Johnson's suspension.

The firing of Phillips and Walsh was as inevitable as the trading of Johnson. Phillips and his coaches—Pete Reiser, Norm Sherry, Rocky Bridges and Fred Koenig—got the word on October 7, when Autry announced that a move had to be made for the good of team morale.

Phillips refused to blast Walsh for his lack of support. "Too much has been said already this year," he said. "I feel I did the best job I could considering what I had to work with and the circumstances that surrounded the season."

Autry again cited team morale (several players had said they would ask to be traded if Walsh remained) when he announced on October 21 that Walsh was being terminated with four years remaining on his contract.

Walsh would reflect on the traumatic summer of 1971 and say, "It's impossible to describe what it was like to live through." He said his greatest regret was in not trading Johnson after his batting title of 1970, "but he had played like hell during the final month of that year and I thought he had seen the light, that he would take pride in the batting title and continue to play that way. I should have known there are no panaceas for the Alex Johnsons. He strained the relationship between himself and the other players, between the players and the manager, between the manager and myself.''

Of his failure to intervene, Walsh said, ''My philosophy is that until a player signs his contract, he's the general manager's responsibility. After he signs, he belongs to the manager. The more the front office interferes in the clubhouse, the more likely the chance of morale problems.

''I stepped into the Johnson situation only after Lefty came to me and said he'd had it. We were in Oakland and I said, 'OK, have him in my room this afternoon.'

''I talked for an hour with Alex and he promised to give 100%. At the same time, Lefty was holding a clubhouse meeting during which he told the team that Alex would never again play for the Angels. I couldn't understand Lefty's reasoning, since he'd just asked me to sit down with Alex and see if I might have some influence. At any rate, I asked that he be returned to the lineup.''

Those words set the stage, eventually, for what even Walsh conceded was a lie, a lie that convinced Autry a change would have to be made.

Walsh said at the time of the Ruiz incident that he had no evidence a gun was employed. He then stated under oath at the grievance hearing that a gun had been used, prompting Autry to tell reporters he was stunned by his general manager's failure to advise him of all the facts.

''I had known Ruiz had a gun,'' Walsh said, ''but I did not know if he had threatened Johnson with it, and since Ruiz was not a U.S. citizen, I felt it would jeopardize his status to admit there was a gun.

''I gave this information to the commissioner and to the American League president. I also called Autry, but when I was told he wasn't available, I gave the information to Bob Reynolds. I asked Bob to relay it to Gene, but I can only assume Reynolds didn't do it or Autry forgot having talked to Reynolds.''

There is this certainty even a decade later: Neither Autry, nor the organization, nor the man who succeeded Dick Walsh, will ever forget what was expected to be the ''new era.''

Chapter
XII

NEW ERA II was less traumatic than its predecessor, but no more successful. The professional in whose hands Autry entrusted it this time was Harry I. Dalton, who left a position as director of player personnel with the Baltimore Orioles to become executive vice president and general manager of the Angels.

Dalton served in that capacity for six years, during which time the Angels employed five field managers, never finished higher than fourth and never even reached .500, getting closest in 1973, when the record was 79-83.

The new general manager took over a dispirited organization sadly in need of stability, one that required rebuilding from the ground up. Dalton needed time and Autry gave it to him, extending his original five-year contract.

The task was made more difficult by a new wave of injuries and misfortune, the plague that has haunted the Angels since their inception. Dalton resisted predictions and refused to em-

ploy the traditional cliché, the stock and solemn pronounce-
ment of a Five Year Plan.

Scouting director Walter Shannon and a number of men who
had worked under Shannon and Dalton in Baltimore joined the
California migration. The farm system took on a new look. A
trickle of potential players appeared. A few made it. A few
made it elsewhere. The majority failed.

Dalton was accessible to club and city officials and did not
share Walsh's fear that a general manager's presence in the
clubhouse would lead to morale problems. He visited the clubhouse before and after almost every game, making himself
accessible to the players and manager.

The Angels reacquired the look and feel of a major league
organization—everywhere except on the field. Dalton's inability to find the man he perceived as the right manager seemed
an indictment of his ability to judge character and an attempt
to shift responsibility for the club's poor performance, making
a scapegoat of the man on the field.

The hirings and firings became an annual rite, serving, in
some measure, to dilute a reputation Dalton had established
with Baltimore, where, in his six seasons as personnel director, the Orioles won four American League pennants and two
World Championships.

Dalton, 43 at the time of his hiring by the Angels, had spent
18 years with the Orioles following graduation from Amherst
College. He was an assistant farm director before becoming
farm director, then personnel director. Autry and Reynolds
pursued him vigorously, making an initial contact in September of 1971, during the final days of the Walsh nightmare.

Autry, in fact, probed Dalton's interest before asking the
Orioles for permission to talk with him, raising the ire of Baltimore's then owner, Jerold Hoffberger, who rejected the
formal request when it came just prior to his team's confron-
tation with Oakland in the American League's championship
series.

Autry waited until after the World Series, in which Pittsburgh defeated Baltimore, and then called again. This time he
received the owner's approval, though grudgingly.

"What difference does it make?" Hoffberger said in an in-

terview with the *Los Angeles Times*. "They talked to him once
without my permission and I assume they'd do it again.

"I turned them down the first time because it was right
before the playoffs and Series, and Harry had important obli-
gations to the club and to our fans, but it would be wrong for
me to stand in his way now. He knows how I feel. He knows
how badly I want him to remain with the Orioles."

Dalton would laugh at that. He would reflect later and say
Hoffberger had given him no clue as to how he felt, that when
he asked permission to meet with the Angels, Hoffberger
made no attempt to talk him out of it. Dalton admitted he was
hurt by that. He said it made him feel as if his 18 years spent
helping to construct a successful organization had been unap-
preciated.

The Orioles left for a tour of Japan two days after the World
Series ended, but Dalton flew to California and met with
Autry, Reynolds and attorney Clair Stout at Lakeside Country
Club in Los Angeles, outlining the prospective job.

He then returned to Baltimore, at which time Hoffberger
said he would be willing to give Dalton the same title the
Angels would, meaning that Dalton would receive a raise and
assume complete authority over the Orioles' operation, an authority he formally shared with Frank Cashen, a management
expert from Hoffberger's National Brewery Company.

The offer came too late to dissuade Dalton, who had wanted
to hear it a week earlier. He returned to California on the
following Saturday and met with Autry in Palm Springs, putting the finishing touches on a contract calling for $75,000 a
year.

Dalton called Hoffberger and told him he had decided to
leave, forsaking a championship team in favor of a team that
had never won a championship and seemed unlikely to win
one soon. That alone, he said, was a significant part of the
Angels' attraction, the opportunity and challenge to develop
another winner. Dalton said he was also attracted by a significant increase in salary, by his belief that the Anaheim area
could become one of the league's best, and by the affection
that wife Pat and their three daughters shared for the West
Coast.

"As one of the architects of the Orioles' success," Robert Reynolds said, "Dalton is used to winning. After the disappointment of last summer, we are determined to build a winner."

Dalton's hiring was officially announced on October 27. The new general manager said it would probably be several weeks before a manager was hired, since his first obligation was to analyze the organization's playing talent. His first trade then came before the hiring of his first manager.

Attending baseball's winter meetings in Phoenix, Dalton sent relief pitcher Dave LaRoche to Minnesota for shortstop Leo Cardenas, whose age was somewhere between 33 and 43 and who had set a major league record in 1971 for fewest errors in a season.

The Angels would learn that Cardenas didn't make many errors because he didn't reach many balls. The disheartening discovery would be made during the ensuing summer, after Jim Fregosi, made expendable by the acquisition of Cardenas, had also been traded.

"In 11 years the Angels have never finished higher than third," Dalton said, attempting to explain the acquisition of Cardenas and the availability of Fregosi. "I believe Fregosi [who had undergone foot surgery in 1971] can still be productive, but I'm determined to put the 25 best players in uniform.

"We had to have a shortstop and now we've achieved one of our objectives. Our bullpen is a little thin [LaRoche had a 5-1 record and 9 saves in 1971], but it is much easier to develop a relief pitcher than a shortstop."

Dalton would find that it was not easy to do either. The Angels had critical problems both at shortstop and in the bullpen during the 1972 season, making the job of new manager Del Rice almost impossible.

Cardenas was acquired on December 1, 1971, kicking off a two-week period in which the Angels dominated the headlines.

December 6: Forty days and 40 nights after his own hiring, Dalton hired Rice as the Angels' third manager. The job had been offered to no one else, though an attempt had been made to negotiate with Yankee manager Ralph Houk.

Responding to Autry's urging, Dalton had called Yankee general manager Lee MacPhail, who refused to give the Angels permission to talk with Houk. MacPhail also told Dalton that Houk would not be interested in joining the Angels.

Dalton then turned to Rice, 49, the 17-year major league catcher who had been the first player ever signed by the Angels. Rice spent only the one year on the club's player roster before joining Bill Rigney's coaching staff for five years. He went on to manage at virtually every stop in the Angels' farm system and was elevated to the job he "had always wanted" after guiding Salt Lake City to the Pacific Coast League pennant, being named Minor League Manager of the Year by *The Sporting News.*

"His managerial record is excellent," Dalton said. "In four years in that capacity, he's sent nine players to the majors with a possibility of four or five more next spring. He is a firm, knowledgeable leader who fits our needs completely."

If there was one other consideration, it was this: With the organization coming off a series of three disruptive seasons, Dalton felt it would be beneficial to stability and unity, to the organization's shattered morale, if the new manager came from within. Hell's Angels became Del's Angels, though a year later Dalton's posture had changed dramatically. No longer was Rice the "firm, knowledgeable leader who fits our needs completely."

December 8: The Angels announced a coaching staff of Peanuts Lowrey, Tom Morgan, John Roseboro and Bobby Winkles, the latter having decided to give up the security of his position as baseball coach at Arizona State to pursue the goal of a managerial position in the majors.

Winkles, 41, had spent 13 years at Arizona State, winning NCAA championships in 1965, 1967 and 1969 while compiling a career record of 524-173. Among his pro products were Reggie Jackson, Rick Monday and Sal Bando.

"I suppose," Winkles said, "that some players might be leery of a college coach, but I'll accept the challenge. I'm sure that by the end of spring training they'll all admit that Winkles knows baseball. They'll all realize that to be a successful college coach, it can't be otherwise. You have to know every phase of the game. You're it. You don't have a staff with specialized instructors."

Winkles had known Rice for almost ten years, but it was

Dalton who lobbied for the hiring of a man who had received pro offers virtually every year while at Arizona State, but never previously had the opportunity to step in at the major league level.

"I didn't hire Bobby on the basis that he was the heir apparent," Dalton said, "nor was I trying to be a pioneer. Bobby had a solid reputation for instruction and fundamentals, and I believed that with a young organization his enthusiasm would rub off. I saw him as the perfect complement for Del."

Winkles would become more than a complement. He would become the manager, a position in which he heard few compliments.

December 11: Jim Fregosi, the six-time All-Star and only remaining Angel from the 1961 expansion draft, was traded to the Mets for pitcher Nolan Ryan, outfielder Lee Stanton, pitcher Don Rose and catcher Francisco Estrada.

Fregosi, the clubhouse leader and unnamed captain, said he was a better player than Cardenas and that he was traded only because Dalton wanted to sever ties to the past and establish his authority.

Dalton said Fregosi was traded because he did not believe the shortstop could regain his mobility after the foot surgery of 1971 and he had the chance to acquire one of baseball's best arms.

"Sure," Fregosi said, "I'll be leaving some of my heart behind, but after last year this is the perfect year to make the move. It's obvious the Angels didn't want me and I'm happy to go.

"I'll be playing for a pennant contender and that's what I've always wanted. I'll be playing for fans who get excited and emotional. I can concentrate on playing baseball. I don't always have to be the man in the middle."

Regardless of motivations, it proved to be Dalton's best trade for several reasons:

—Fregosi, who would return to the Angels in another time and another capacity, went on to demonstrate Dalton had been right, that he had lost mobility and that his best years *were* behind him.

—The fringe players proved useful. Stanton supplied a degree of power during years otherwise almost devoid of it, and Rose was traded to the Giants in 1973 for pitcher Ed Figueroa, who won 16 games for the Angels in 1975 and was then traded to the Yankees for a bona fide power hitter, Bobby Bonds.

—Ryan soon lived up to his awesome potential, producing a string of high-strikeout and low-hit games that did not always result in victories, since he was a consistent victim of poor support. He created a volume of new records and became an authentic gate attraction, attaining a plateau comparable with Anaheim's other folk hero, the celebrated Mickey Mouse.

The civic wounds were still festering in the winter following Walsh's firing, and Dalton tried other means to bind the breach and regenerate interest. He hired former Dodgers and Cincinnati Reds executive Tom Seeberg as director of community relations and initiated an "Industrial Caravan" on which club executives and players visited businesses and industries in the Anaheim area.

The Angels were a hit at every stop, drawing crowds that often exceeded those they drew during a season in which attendance dipped to 744,190, the all-time low in Anaheim. Ryan worked only once every fourth or fifth day. In between, the crowds averaged 5,000 to 10,000 less than when Ryan was scheduled.

The nightmare of 1971 was over, but the disintegration continued in 1972. The Angels finished fifth, 18 games behind Oakland. They finished with a 75-80 record, having never been at or over .500 after the second week of the season when they lost five in a row, including four straight to Texas, a series, Dalton said, that "put us on the wrong road for the rest of the year."

Rice talked of having the best pitching staff he had ever been associated with and then saw injuries restrict the availability of Ryan, Wright and Messersmith during the first half, after which the four-man rotation that also embraced Rudy May compiled a 1.80 ERA over the last two months.

Each of the four starters finished with an earned run average under 3.00, but each was handicapped by an offense that produced only 78 home runs and averaged fewer than three runs per game.

It might have been even worse had Dalton not negotiated a May trade in which pitcher Tom Murphy went to Kansas City for first baseman Bob Oliver, who led the Angels with 20 homers and 76 RBI.

Cardenas batted only .223 and considered driving through a cemetery with his bats in the trunk of his car so as to chase out the evil spirits that had wormed their way into the wood.

Messersmith, the 20-game winner of 1971, suffered a broken finger early and won only 8 games. The bullpen, known as the Arson Squad in future seasons because of its inflammatory performances, challenged the ineffectiveness of the offense by saving only 16 games.

Rice frequently brought his team out early—sometimes as early as nine in the morning—in an attempt to review fundamentals and awaken the offense, but the only real spark in an otherwise lethargic season came from Ryan's arm.

The right-hander, whose fast ball was timed at 100.9 miles per hour by scientists from Rockwell International, won 19 games and lost 16. He had a 1-hitter, two 2-hitters, four 3-hitters and four 4-hitters. He registered 329 strikeouts, the fourth highest total ever. His 1-hitter against Boston included 8 straight strikeouts, an American League record. He also tied a record in that game by striking out the side on 9 pitches.

Ryan also issued 157 walks that season, hounded again by the control problems that have plagued his career. Now, however, he had begun to learn how to use that wildness to his advantage. He had become baseball's most intimidating pitcher. Reggie Jackson was among the many who said Ryan was the only pitcher he was afraid of. Many sought refuge, a night off, by claiming they were victims of the Ryan flu, an illness that conveniently appeared when Ryan was scheduled to work.

Ryan delivered 18 wild pitches in 1972, enough to keep the bravest of hitters on their toes. He also displayed the low-key, easygoing, unaffected style and personality that made him a favorite of the media.

Amid the luxury cars in the players' parking lot, Ryan's truck seemed out of place. He wore jeans and boots before it was the thing to do. A Texan who loved the places and spaces of his native state, he loathed New York, both from a stand-point of environment and what he said was a lack of help and support offered by Mets manager Gil Hodges and pitching coach Rube Walker.

The Mets' rotation, Ryan said, was designed strictly for Tom Seaver. It was Seaver, and Seaver alone, Ryan said, who worked every fourth day. A hard-throwing young pitcher with control problems, with a weekend-a-month military obliga-tion, found it difficult getting the consistent work and assis-tance required for his proper development.

There were moments, Ryan conceded, when he considered quitting, periods when he didn't believe there was a future. The trade, he said, came at a propitious time.

Ryan found in Anaheim a more comfortable pace, a lifestyle to which he could adjust. It wasn't his ranch, but it also wasn't the New York jungle. He also got the chance that wasn't al-ways provided by the Mets, the opportunity to come back from a start that might include seven walks, two wild pitches and a hit batter.

Manager Rice, pitching coach Tom Morgan and catcher Jeff Torborg worked constantly with Ryan, who would say later, "I don't know how to thank them for the chance they gave me. I may not have always made the most of the opportunity. I may not have had the ability to do so. But at least they gave me the chance that everyone is entitled to."

Morgan was of particular help, providing Ryan with a sense of rhythm and timing, a delivery with which he could make best use of his comparatively short, muscular legs, his base of power. Morgan was Ryan's pitching coach for three years, after which Ryan continued to seek his help and advice in a clandestine manner, making either phone calls or visits to the Morgan home.

Ryan reflected on a career that would take him to the Hall of Fame and said 1972 was the turning point. It was in 1972, his first year with the Angels, that he became convinced he could win in the major leagues, certain he could support his family through baseball. He will always regard that otherwise undistinguished summer with more affection than Del Rice, of whom Ryan said, "He was a good manager with a bad team."

The season ended at the same time as Rice's one-year contract. His rehiring was clouded by uncertainty. He conceded that there were things he would do differently if given another chance.

"I hadn't seen most of the guys play regularly before," he said. "Through the course of the season I learned a great deal about them. If we were to go back to spring training I'd probably be stricter in a number of areas. We ran the bases poorly, for example, and our bunting was even worse.

"These are things you learn only by watching people play. I couldn't guess in the spring that some veterans would be the worst offenders.

"On the whole, I'm satisfied with the job I did. Under the circumstances I don't see how I could have done anything differently. We simply didn't score many runs. And yet, if we have Andy Messersmith healthy, winning 15 to 20 games instead of going 8 and 11, we're right in the thick of it.

"I'm a patient man and I can only hope that Dalton is, too."

Hope was all there was for Rice. "I'm disappointed," Dalton said. "I thought we were capable of playing over .500 and scoring more runs. We also didn't play very good fundamental baseball. We missed cutoff men, threw to the wrong base and ran poorly. We failed to do a lot of things that don't show in the box scores."

It added up to a pink slip for Rice—a firing, Dalton said, that was in Rice's best interest, since his health had deteriorated during the long season, his customary Scotch and water replaced by milk and Maalox.

"Del had lost control of the club some," Dalton said, "but I'm not sure we'd have made the change if it hadn't been for his health. He was a classic ulcer case. We had to make a change both for the club's and for Del's best interest."

One year into the job and now looking for his second manager, Dalton had only just begun.

Chapter
XIII

IN CONSIDERING a successor to Rice, owner Autry investigated the availability of Oakland manager Dick Williams. Autry received permission from As owner Charles Finley to talk with Williams, who was still basking in the glow of a World Championship. Williams had one year left on his contract and told Autry he wasn't interested in a move.

On October 12, 1972, less than one year since he had left Arizona State, Bobby Winkles became the first man in baseball history to receive a major league managerial job after having previously managed only at the college level.

In reflection, Autry said, "Harry and I both felt it was something of a gamble to give the job to a man with so little experience, but we also felt that because of his rapport with the young players and his reputation as an instructor, he might give the club a real spark.

"Walter Alston had great success with the Dodgers after a big league career that consisted of one at-bat. Joe McCarthy never played in the majors but was a legend as manager of the Cubs and Yankees.

"We believed in Bobby and felt he could pull it off. I still believe he might have except that he was a victim of one of those no-win situations. We acquired Frank Robinson, who had been a great player in both leagues and whose goal was to become a manager, a position no black had yet attained. Robinson reached his goal [with Cleveland in 1975], but before that, some thought he was managing the Angels. Many of our players went to Frank instead of Winkles, and there was growing friction and tension."

The hostile atmosphere eventually forced the Angels to make another managerial move, but that was not until midseason of 1974. Of Winkles' appointment, Dalton said, "The fact that at times there was a noticeable lack of enthusiasm [last year] was an important factor in my decision. I don't expect a constant rah-rah attitude, but when you're playing 162 games there has to be an unbroken thread of determination. I don't think Bobby's enthusiasm and aggressiveness can be challenged. Winning is in his background. Some people will say that college is different, but I feel that baseball is baseball."

Winkles' hiring became known as the "Great Experiment." Some wondered if the third base coach would give signals with pompons and if there would be card stunts between innings. The players called him Joe College and talked about his playbook, 70 mimeographed pages titled "The Winkles System of Playing Baseball."

The new manager initiated hair and dress codes and announced a series of fines for any player showing up a coach or manager. His enthusiasm and drive seemed to win the respect of the Angels, though a frequently unorthodox approach to strategy earned him the nickname "Dr. Strange Moves." The feeling also grew slowly that communication was not one of his strengths, this despite the fact that the Angels seemed to lead the league in meetings.

Among the players who sat in on those meetings were five obtained from the Dodgers in a November, 1972, trade that was the biggest ever between the southern California rivals. It was consummated at the winter meetings in Hawaii, the tropic breezes seeming to soften the hard-line attitudes that the Dodgers and Angels maintained in regard to each other.

The Angels packaged pitcher Andy Messersmith and third baseman Ken McMullen for delivery up the freeway. The Dodgers agreed to exchange pitchers Bill Singer and Mike Strahler, infielders Bobby Valentine and Bill Grabarkewitz and outfielder Frank Robinson, the only man ever to win the Most Valuable Player Award in both leagues.

It was the second time Robinson had been involved in a major trade negotiated by Dalton. The first was in 1966 when Dalton acquired Robinson from Cincinnati in his initial transaction as the Orioles' personnel director. Robinson soon became the cornerstone of the Orioles' dynasty, the Orioles winning pennants in four of the six years he and Dalton were together.

The right fielder hit for average and power, played his position respectably and was the team leader, setting an example via a competitive and aggressive style.

Robinson was also candid and outspoken, and those traits, coupled with the fact that at 37 he had been the victim of a series of leg injuries, restricting his effectiveness and availability in his one year with the Dodgers, led Los Angeles to trade him. It was a trade he had asked for if the Dodgers did not intend to play him regularly.

Dalton had no compunction about taking him back, saying he was convinced that Robinson's pride would enable him to rebound from 1972 and that his leadership qualities were an important consideration. Dalton said he saw Robinson as an adjunct to Winkles and not a rival or threat.

Dalton was right, at least on the matter of Robinson's ability to regain his batting stroke. Used both in the outfield and as a designated hitter, Robinson slugged 30 homers and drove in 97 runs, both club records for a right-handed hitter.

It was a relatively peaceful period for Robinson and Winkles, whose team set club records for hits and batting average en route to finishing fourth in 1973 with a 79-83 record, 15 games behind Oakland.

The Angels were in first place on June 26, but lost 19 of their next 28 games, the absence again of a bullpen and shortstop proving critical. Bobby Valentine, a multi-talented and charismatic prospect, had opened the season at shortstop and was scheduled to play there on the night of May 17 when center fielder Ken Berry came down with the flu, and Winkles responded by shifting Valentine to center. It was an ill-fated decision, for in the fourth inning, chasing a drive hit by Oakland second baseman Dick Green, Valentine leaped against the chain-link fence, caught his right spokes in the webbing, and broke his leg so seriously that his career was ruined. The 27-year-old player was carried off the field on a stretcher and never regained his speed or mobility, joining the long list of jinxed Angels.

Former Dodger teammate Bill Singer proved more fortunate, at least during the 1973 season. A 20-game winner with the Dodgers in 1969, Singer became only the 12th pitcher in baseball history to win 20 games in both leagues, fashioning a record of 20-14. He also combined with Ryan to register 624 strikeouts, breaking a major league record for two pitchers on the same team, a record set in 1965 by the renowned tandem of Sandy Koufax and Don Drysdale.

Ryan pitched complete-game victories in his last seven starts to finish with 21 wins against 16 defeats. It was a season of remarkable accomplishments for the man whose fast ball earned him the nickname "The Express," a takeoff on the movie *Von Ryan's Express*. Ryan became only the fifth pitcher in baseball history to throw two no-hitters in a season. He struck out 12 while no-hitting Kansas City on May 15 and struck out 17 while no-hitting Detroit on July 15. The Tigers' futility was characterized by first baseman Norm Cash, who carried a piano leg as he went to the plate in the late innings.

Incredibly, Ryan should have thrown *four* no-hitters that year, losing two others through fielding mistakes.

In his first start after the no-hitter against Detroit, with a chance to become the only pitcher aside from Johnny VanderMeer to hurl no-hitters in consecutive starts, Ryan kept it alive until the eighth inning when the weak-hitting Baltimore shortstop, Mark Belanger, blooped a single to center, the ball falling just in front of a charging Ken Berry, who, for reasons he couldn't explain, had been playing Belanger as if he were Babe Ruth. It was the only hit Ryan allowed until he lost the game in extra innings.

In an August 30 start against New York, Ryan watched
Thurman Munson loft a first-inning pop-up into shallow center, where second baseman Sandy Alomar and Rudy Meoli
each called for it and then backed off, believing the other
would make the catch. The ball fell for a single, the only hit
Ryan allowed in a 5–0 victory.

Ryan averaged 10.57 strikeouts per nine innings, and joined
Sandy Koufax and Rube Waddell as the only pitchers to record 300 or more strikeouts in consecutive seasons.

He also broke Koufax's single-season record with a total of
383. Ryan got the record in his final start, needing 16 as he
went to work against Minnesota at Anaheim Stadium, where
a crowd of 9,100 offered vocal support on each pitch. He tied
the record by fanning Steve Brye in the eighth inning, tearing
a calf muscle in the process. Trainer Freddie Frederico and
Dr. Jules Rasinski worked on the leg between innings, and
Ryan finally generated enough velocity to claim Rich Reese on
a swinging third strike in the eleventh.

Ryan finished the 1973 season with club records for complete games (26) and innings pitched (326). He led the league
again with 162 walks, 15 wild pitches and 7 hit batters, but he
also boasted an ERA (2.87) that was among the league's best.

It was a disappointment to Ryan that he only finished second
in voting for the Cy Young Award, which went to Baltimore's
Jim Palmer, but he was angered more when Palmer said the
voting was justified because he pitched for putouts while Ryan
pitched only for strikeouts.

"I always thought they were the same thing," Ryan said.

Ryan's feelings were soothed some by a raise to $54,000 and
the gift of a new truck as bonus for his no-hitters. The gener-
osity helped him to retain a confidence and momentum as he
relaxed in the wake of the old season and prepared for the
new.

It was another good season for Ryan in 1974, when he was
22-16, the anemic Angels scoring just 22 runs in his 16 defeats.
The pathetic nature of the Angels' attack was illustrated by
the fact that Ryan had only one win to show for a three-game
streak in which he registered a major league record of 41
strikeouts. He recorded 367 for the year becoming the first
pitcher ever to accumulate 300 or more in three straight sea-

sons, and he hurled his third no-hitter against Minnesota in his final start.

The Angels won their final five games to avoid their worst record ever. As it was, they finished last for the first time, a record of 68-94 leaving them 22 games behind Oakland.

Pitching prospect Bruce Heinbechner was killed in a spring training car accident; Singer, 7-4 in a bid to win 20 again, underwent back surgery in June; and leadoff man Mickey Rivers, a fleet-footed and scatter-brained center fielder (the Angels called him "The Chancellor"), who led the club with a .285 average, missed the last six weeks of the season with a broken hand.

Robinson hit 10 fewer homers and drove in 34 fewer runs and still led the Angels in both departments. He also led the team in intrigue, since he appeared to be at the heart of a deepening clubhouse rift that split the players into those supporting Winkles and those supporting Robinson. A losing season tends to magnify the little things that happen on all clubs, and that seemed to be what happened in 1974, when the suddenly sensitive Robinson said Winkles wasn't communicating with him. Winkles said Dalton wasn't responding to either the growing tension or the manager's recommendations involving players, and the media displayed a tendency to look everywhere except at the lack of talent for reasons surrounding the Angels' poor play.

The absence of a bullpen, the inconsistent nature of the offense, the significant string of injuries—all seemed overlooked amid an epidemic of bruised egos and feelings.

The overriding suspicion was that Robinson, critical of Winkles' communicative and strategic skills, had been attempting to create a situation in which close friend Dalton would ultimately hand him the managerial reins.

Dalton, who watched the situation fester while refusing the peacemaker's role, denied it would ever come to that, and those close to the organization tended to believe him, since it was unlikely that a franchise located in a conservative hotbed such as Orange County would hire the first black manager.

Robinson finally reached a point where he refused to discuss the situation, saying, "I've been made to look like the goat in this whole thing." He had already fueled the flames with a series of public criticisms of Winkles, and he had allowed himself to become involved in a shouting match with the manager in the lobby of a Milwaukee hotel. The public debate stemmed from a clubhouse meeting in which Winkles told the team he had asked Dalton to trade Robinson.

In mid-June, amid the mounting belief that a change was inevitable, Winkles said, "I work for the hardest-working general manager in baseball, but I'm a little disappointed that he's become a middle-of-the-roader with me. I truthfully believed Harry would take a stronger stand about me, one way or the other."

Dalton finally made his stand on June 26, 1974, responding in a manner spelled out on page one of the "General Managers' Manual." He reacted in the way that all general managers have always reacted. He fired the manager.

"It was a mistake on my part to believe he could manage a major league team without more experience," Dalton said. "It was a mistake on my part not to insist that he go to triple A for a year first. Bobby was fine around the kids, but he just wasn't sure of himself with the veterans. He was obviously uncomfortable in Robinson's presence, though I never felt Frank made any covert or overt attempt to undermine him."

Winkles responded with a bitterness that he later expressed regret for, though much of what he said in the initial wake of his firing would be repeated by his successor. "Dalton made all the decisions on players, and I think everybody knew I was uncomfortable with Frank Robinson around," Winkles said. "I admitted openly I couldn't handle him. Maybe they should have fired the general manager. The thing that disappointed me was that he [Dalton] seldom paid any attention to any recommendations. I've always delved into the hearts and souls of my players. I feel I know them better than anybody, including the general manager. But, somehow, Harry and I could never get together on who should be on the ball club." Winkles later said he hadn't meant to put the blame on anyone except himself. "The Robinson situation," he said, "was my own fault. I did a lousy job of handling him. I might have kept my job if I had done a better job. I'm basically a disciplinarian but I didn't have enough discipline. I did a —— —— job."

In his book, *The Other Game* (Waco, Texas: Word Books,

1977), Nolan Ryan told author Bill Libby that there was guilt on both sides. "He [Robinson] tried to manage the Angels while he was playing with them, and he was a disruptive factor on the team. . . . Winkles was a fine person who had been a great manager at Arizona State, but he was not prepared to deal with professionals or to manage in the majors. He knew fundamentals, but he didn't know the players, and he didn't know the majors.

"Winks tried to treat everyone well, but you don't motivate major leaguers with the same rah-rah spirit as you do collegians. We're married men making big money out there, and we play or try to play professionally through a long hard schedule of 162 games, night after night, with few days off. You simply can't sustain a college spirit through that traveling grind.

"Winks insisted on details like the players having short hair and wearing ties on the road. The players merely laughed at him. Today's players wear long hair and mod clothes. I don't, but most do. The rules didn't bother me, except that I saw they bothered most of the others. You can't treat a man like a child and get away with it.

"Whatever their troubles, they turned to Robinson. He's always been a leader, especially among black players. He's a powerful personality, and players have always respected him. I lost a lot of respect for him in that situation. Instead of backing up Bobby, he turned the players against him. Robinson's not a bigot, but because of the situation, he created a black-white rift on the team. He split the team right down the middle, black and white. You were either Robby's player or you were Bobby's."

Dalton had met with Autry and Reynolds on June 15, eleven days before Winkles' firing, and set the wheels in motion. Autry emerged thinking that the club couldn't again go for an untested or second-best manager. He felt he had to have the best, a strong-willed disciplinarian. He and Reynolds flew to Oakland to meet with As owner Charles Finley, seeking permission again to talk with Williams.

It had been almost two years since they last talked. Williams had become fed up with the phone calls in the middle of the night, the middle of the game, the constant interference from a dictatorial owner who believed he knew more than his managers about selecting a lineup and roster. Williams received a managerial offer from the New York Yankees and attempted to accept it. He believed Finley would let him out of a contract that had a year to run, since Finley had said as much on national TV after the 1973 World Series.

Williams' belief was misplaced. There was no way to predict Finley's thinking, no matter what he said, a fact Williams discovered again when the As' owner went to court in an effort to block Williams' bid to manage the Yankees. The result was a long litigation which ended with Bill Virdon being named to manage New York, Alvin Dark becoming manager of the As and Williams, still receiving paychecks from Finley, going to work for multimillionaire John D. McArthur, a Florida insurance and real estate mogul. Williams' primary job was to address businessmen on the art of motivation, a subject with which he was familiar, since in six years as a major league manager with Boston and Oakland he had led his teams to two world titles, three American League pennants and three divisional crowns.

Finley, who viewed his managers as nothing more than middlemen and always believed he could find another manager on the next street corner, had obstructed Williams' move to the Yankees more out of a distaste for the Yankees than an anger over Williams' desire to leave the As. He sat in an Oakland bar with the owners of the Angels for more than six hours, talking about everything except the reason for their trip. He then finally told them that since they had been supportive of his decision to move the As out of Kansas City, he would give them permission to talk with Williams.

Autry agreed to give the As $50,000 in compensation if Williams accepted his offer, which he did. Williams signed a three-and-a-half-year contract at $100,000 a year and took the reins of the Angels on July 1, 1974.

That night, in an obvious bid for unity on a divided team, Williams appointed Robinson as his captain, the first captain in the Angels' history.

"I'm glad Dick has this much faith in me," Robinson said.

"Now I can give advice to somebody without thinking, 'Am I doing the right thing?' "

There was little Robinson or Williams could do to stop the Angels' tailspin. The season's pattern had been set. Too many players had stopped caring. Too many had been injured. There was no relief—in either the bullpen or the farm system. The Angels lost their first 10 games under Dick Williams, waived Robinson to Cleveland in September and finished the year with a 36-48 record under their new manager.

Tom Morgan, Salty Parker and John Roseboro were released as coaches and replaced by Jerry Adair, Billy Muffett and Grover Resinger, Williams' first lieutenant. Whitey Herzog, later a successful manager of the Kansas City Royals, remained as third base coach. Williams also retained Jimmie Reese, whose baseball career started in 1917 when he was hired as a batboy with the Los Angeles Angels of the Pacific Coast League. At 69, he was a former roommate of Babe Ruth, the game's foremost exponent of the fungo bat, and a confidant and friend to Nolan Ryan.

The off-season's boldest move—the club's only move, really—was made by Autry, who responded to Robert Reynolds' decision to leave the organization by initiating a search for a new club president, a man who would be on the job full-time, giving the Angels a more visible face in the community, taking some of the administrative load off Dalton and inaugurating a more marketable program of promotions and public relations.

Autry sought the advice of several people, including Arthur (Red) Patterson, longtime vice president of the Dodgers and a public relations specialist acknowledged to be the father of many of today's most popular promotions, such as Bat Day, Ball Day and the Oldtimers Game.

Autry called Patterson in midwinter to ask his opinion on three people: St. Louis Cardinals vice president Richard Meyer, former Cincinnati Reds owner Bill DeWitt, and A. Ray Smith, a Tulsa oilman who owned the minor league club in that city and was a lifelong friend of Autry's.

The cowboy listened to Patterson's opinions, thanked him for his help and hung up. Patterson thought about the conversation, then told club president Peter O'Malley about it.

"Hell," O'Malley said, "what he's really asking is, 'Are *you* interested?' I hate the thought of losing you, but it's the chance of a lifetime. Call him back."

Patterson shook his head, finding O'Malley's interpretation of Autry's call hard to believe. He returned to his office, thought about it some more, then made the call.

"I know that I just attempted to answer your question," he said to Autry, "but, in thinking more about it, I realized that I had interest in the job myself and wondered if we could talk about it."

Autry and Patterson met at Lakeside Country Club the next morning and reached an agreement within five minutes. The announcement was made that night at the Baseball Writers Association banquet. Patterson and Dalton insisted they could work together, though Patterson, as club president, would be kept aware of Dalton's moves and serve as a liaison with Autry.

"Harry will develop the product and I'll help sell it," said Patterson, who at 65 had the energy of a man of 35, a devoted baseball executive who thought nothing of delivering three speeches a day, and of whom it was once said, "He could sell snowballs to the Eskimos."

Patterson received the same $75,000-a-year salary as Dalton and a contract that covered the same number of years. The Angels had drawn 917,269 in 1974 and Patterson said, "If there are fifty guys in Hemet or Encino who are potential ticket buyers, I'm going. I'll quit if we ever draw less than a million again."

Williams made a comparable promise. Remarkably self-confident and a disciple of Dr. Norman Vincent Peale's, the guru of positive thinking, Williams held a team meeting on the opening day of spring training in 1975 and said, "I guarantee you that as long as I'm the manager, you will never again finish last."

Among the believers was Nolan Ryan. "There's a pride and stability here that's never been here before," he said.

The pitcher would eventually have other things to say about Williams, but March is a time of optimism and high hopes, a rose-colored time in which it is impossible to believe that the spring flowers will ever wilt.

The Angels had decided to dedicate the 1975 season to new growth, to the budding flowers of a farm system that had always seemed more like a wasteland.

Among the relatively untested starters were first baseman Bruce Bochte (signed in 1972, Dalton's first year), second baseman Jerry Remy (signed in 1971, Dick Walsh's last year), shortstop Orlando Ramirez (1972) and third baseman Dave Chalk (1972).

The "Incubator Infield" was a classic example of force-feeding, an attempt, some said, by Dalton to prove that his farm system was in gear and producing. It seemed to be Dalton's only real course, since he had little to trade, and it might have been a profitable one had the entire organization not been burdened with the futility of the past, the pressure to win immediately. The players felt it, the manager felt it, the general manager felt it. Time, patience and consistent run production were in short supply.

Mickey Rivers led the league in 1975 with 70 stolen bases, and the Angels stole a total of 220, the most by any team since 1916, but the bats consistently had trouble getting the legs home from second. The Angels hit a league low 55 homers as Williams finished under .500 for the first time in his managerial career and failed to fulfill his spring training promise.

A 72-89 record left the Angels last again, 25½ games behind the As, Williams' former team. The powder-puff attack prompted Texas manager Billy Martin to say that the Angels could take batting practice in a hotel lobby and not break anything. Boston pitcher Bill Lee picked up on that theme after a May victory in Anaheim, saying, "Now I know the Angels could take batting practice in a hotel lobby and not break the chandelier."

Williams decided to put that to a test. He purchased a supply of plastic bats and balls and conducted batting practice in the lobby of the Sheraton-Boston on May 24. The Angels damaged nothing except their own reputation, which suffered yet another blow that night when Lee shut them out, 6-0.

"He popped off and backed it up," Williams said. "He embarrassed the hell out of us."

It was nothing that the Angels couldn't do to themselves. The arson squad saved only 16 games, and four shortstops combined to make 50 errors. Lee Stanton led the club with 14 homers, and no one hit more than .285.

The inconsistency of the offense and defense served to dilute a relatively strong performance by the pitching rotation. Rookie Ed Figueroa won an unanticipated 16 games. Sophomore Frank Tanana, a 14-game winner as a rookie, was 16-9, led the majors in strikeouts with 269, tied a league record for left-handers by striking out 17 Texas batters on June 21 and had a stylish earned run average of 2.62.

The son of a Detroit cop, Tanana was the Angels' No. 1 draft choice in 1971, the year Walsh also signed second baseman Remy and a modestly successful third baseman, Ron Jackson.

Tanana made it first, a cocky left-hander who considered himself without equal, on or off the field. The numbers in his black book were believed to be as impressive as those that followed his name on the statistics sheet.

"I went to an all-boys high school and now I'm making up for it," Tanana said.

He also said, "My idol as a kid was myself," and, "My ambition is to become the best pitcher in baseball. I may have already achieved it."

Tanana was definitely the Angels' best pitcher in 1975, this despite the fact that Nolan Ryan earned a $3,000 bonus and tied Sandy Koufax's career record by hurling his fourth no-hitter on June 1, dispatching Baltimore, 1–0.

Ryan again flirted with the VanderMeer feat by pitching 5⅔ hitless innings against Milwaukee in his next start. He emerged with a two-hit, 6–0, victory, the no-hitter having expired when home run king Henry Aaron, then 41 and a .200 hitter in the twilight of his distinguished career, singled cleanly to right field.

Ryan was 11-3 with that win, but he won only 3 of his last 12 decisions while suffering a series of arm and leg injuries. Ryan's string of three straight seasons with 300 or more strikeouts ended when he struck out only 186.

The frustrating summer came to an appropriate close when four Oakland pitchers combined to no-hit the Angels in the last game, after which Ryan entered the hospital for the removal of bone chips from his right elbow.

Dalton put the Angels under x-ray that winter and decided that a philosophy transplant was needed. It had been the general manager's theory that Anaheim Stadium wasn't conducive to power, that his club should be built on pitching, speed and defense.

Now, suddenly, in the wake of the season in which the Angels had hit just 55 home runs, he went the other way.

Figueroa and Rivers, two players who rose above the mediocrity that surrounded them in 1975, were traded to the Yankees for right-fielder Bobby Bonds, a player with superstar ability and only the fifth major leaguer ever to hit 30 home runs and steal 30 bases in the same season.

Dalton also traded first baseman Jim Spencer and outfielder Morris Nettles to the White Sox for third baseman Bill Melton, the American League's home run leader in 1971 and a man who had not hit less than 15 homers in any of the past three seasons.

Williams sized up his team in spring training of 1976, overlooked the continued absence of a bullpen, dismissed the absence of a replacement for Figueroa and said it was the best he had ever managed, better than the championship clubs of Oakland and Boston.

Williams' textbook case of spring fever was compounded by the fact that he also overlooked the jinx, the curse, the hex—the mysterious spell that had gripped the Angels from the start and could be counted on to strike again in 1976.

Bonds was the victim this time, injuring the middle finger of his right hand when he collided with Dodgers catcher Steve Yeager in an April 3 exhibition game.

Bonds, determined to give the Angels what they had traded for, continued to play, but was unable to generate his customary power. He ultimately underwent surgery in August and finished the year with just 10 home runs and 54 RBI, both, surprisingly, club highs.

Melton, too, was injured early, pulling a leg muscle in April. He appeared in only 118 games and hit just 6 homers, with 42 RBI and a .208 average.

The anticipated power wasn't there as the Angels batted a league low .235 and increased their home run production by a modest 8. Tanana had another fine season (19-10 with a 2.44 ERA), and Ryan came back from surgery to win 17 games (he lost 18) and lead baseball in strikeouts (327) and walks (183), yet that was virtually all there was: "Tanana, Ryan and a lot of cryin'," an apt theme authored by Dave Distel of the *Los Angeles Times*.

The Angels finished fourth with a 76-86 record, 14 games behind Kansas City. Williams was there for only half of it, having been fired on July 23 with a year remaining on his contract.

Dalton removed his third manager in four and a half years because he believed Williams "wasn't ready to come to grips with the needs of a young club. His frustration grew amid adversity. He reached a point where he didn't believe in the organization, the talent or the system. He put so much pressure on the young players that they were unable to be themselves. And he reached a point where he felt he was above the losses, that they tainted him personally."

"I learned a lesson," said Williams, who went on to manage the Montreal Expos. "I learned that you take a hard look at an organization's talent before you jump at their offer. The Angels came after me with a contract that allowed me to become the first six-figure manager. I jumped at it instead of waiting to analyze what they had and what kind of a job I could do with it. It wasn't until later, until I had spent a considerable time asking players to do things they weren't capable of doing, that I realized the only player of substance was Remy and the only pitchers were Ryan and Tanana. It was a great place to work, but they didn't have any players."

And Dalton, Williams believed, didn't respond to the needs, to his field manager's requests for changes. It was a charge similar to that delivered by predecessor Winkles.

"There were never any serious arguments," Williams said, "but the fact that Autry had hired me, that I wasn't really Harry's man, didn't help at all. We weren't as close as we should have been. There wasn't the communication there should have been."

In June of 1976, with Autry in New York on business, Williams and former Dodger teammate Don Drysdale, then a member of the Angels' broadcasting team, had attempted a palace coup. They visited Autry in his suite at the Waldorf-Astoria and recommended Dalton be fired, saying he wasn't responsive to the needs of his manager or club. They suggested Drysdale be moved into an executive capacity.

A man who places a high premium on loyalty, Autry's response to the visit was negative. He listened to both, told them he would discuss the situation with Dalton, and then invited them to leave, only the distaste remaining. Autry, in fact, carried it with him until 1980 when, executives at Golden West Broadcasters say, it was a significant reason that KMPC did not meet Drysdale's contract demands. A year later, faced with the possible loss of advertising revenue in response to lower ratings, Autry relented and rehired Drysdale. The owner was not making as many changes in the broadcasting booth as in the manager's office.

Williams, a self-confessed sore loser, dug his grave in another way, putting relentless pressure on the young Angels while failing to restrain his drill instructor, Grover Resinger, whose intensity was such that he often walked the streets until daybreak after a losing night game.

Williams and Resinger would storm at the Angels in the dugout, and Resinger would often be up on the top step, responding to mistakes by screaming at the young players even before they got off the field.

"They should wear swastikas on their collars," ex-Angel Joe Lahoud said after being traded.

In his book, *The Other Game,* Ryan told author Libby that Williams was sarcastic and very hard to play for. "Dick was always ridiculing his players behind their backs, but they'd hear about it, and they hated him for it. If he wanted to tell them off face to face, he did it in front of the other players as if to embarrass them. I know he won a pennant at Boston, but those tactics turned the players against him before long, and he was fired. He won pennants and championships at Oakland, but anyone who plays for Charlie Finley is used to tough tactics. They were tough, experienced players, anyway, and they won for Williams, but I think they would have won in spite of anyone.

"We had scared, inexperienced players; they didn't play for Dick and didn't win with him. He is good at the game, but bad with young players. He murdered our morale."

The catalyst in Williams' firing was an incident on a bus carrying the Angels from the Los Angeles airport to Anaheim Stadium in the early hours of July 23.

The team was 20 games under .500 and coming off a long road trip. The frustrated Williams, sitting in the front of the bus, reacted to singing and laughter by turning and saying, "Quiet all you winners."

"—— you," responded a voice.

"Who said that?" demanded Williams.

"I did, you ——," said Bill Melton, meeting his manager in the middle of the bus as coaches and players attempted to separate them.

"You're suspended," Williams said.

"This is the happiest day of my life," responded Melton, who ultimately drew a three-day suspension and the congratulations of his teammates for having made the key contribution of his injury-riddled season.

Williams was fired that afternoon and replaced by coach Norm Sherry, whose relaxed, low-key style was in direct contrast to the authoritative Williams.

"We had reached the point," the new manager said, "where we couldn't do anything right. The players were trying so hard to please Dick that they were putting the monkey on their backs. Dick's from the old school. It was just his way.

"At the first meeting, I told the players not to worry about pleasing me. I said, 'You'll make mistakes and so will I, but if we can cut down on the number of mistakes we'll make progress.' They had to stop thinking a pop-up or error or wild pitch was the end of the world."

The Angels responded with a 37-29 record over the second half and Sherry was rewarded on October 4 with a one-year contract, becoming the Angels' sixth manager and the first under the game's new rules. Baseball became moneyball in the winter of 1976, and Gene Autry demonstrated he knew how to play.

Chapter
XIV

ON THE eve of spring training in 1977, Norm Sherry thought back to July 23 of 1976, the day he replaced Dick Williams as manager. It was an off day for the Angels, and Sherry had just returned home from taking his family to the beach.

The phone rang at 4 P.M. "Can you get right down to the stadium?" Red Patterson asked.

"Anything wrong?" Sherry was worried.

"Yes, but not with you," Patterson said.

Sherry arrived at the park and found the doors locked.

"I had to pound away for about ten minutes before I caught someone's attention. When I finally got upstairs, Red handed me a press release. I had just started to read it when Tom Seeberg came into the room and said, 'It's on the air.'

" 'What's on the air?' I asked him.

"Then I read on and found out I was the manager. I never had a chance to say no, as if I would have. I'm still pinching myself about that, let alone the caliber of team I now have."

Sherry would enter the 1977 season as manager of a team favored to win the American League West. It was suddenly as if there had never been a string of futile and frustrating summers. The Angels may never have finished higher than third, and may have finished better than .500 only four times in sixteen years, but it was as if 1977 represented a fresh start, the start certainly of something big.

The great expectations stemmed from a decision by Gene Autry, exasperated by the failure to farm his own winner, to contribute to the economic revolution that swept baseball in the winter of 1976.

Freed by historic changes in the game's reserve system, many of the top stars celebrated the country's bicentennial by playing out the option year of their contracts and declaring their independence. They then became available to the highest bidder through a free agent reentry draft that became an annual event.

The procedure sent salaries soaring, as owner after owner displayed a predictable lack of restraint in the bid to buy a pennant.

Autry drove in from his Palm Springs hotel in October of 1976 to have lunch with Dalton and Patterson and discuss what role, if any, the Angels would take.

"Gene was against the whole concept," Dalton said. "He knew what effect it would have. But when he asked me if I felt our restraint would help create restraint throughout the game, I had to answer negatively. I told him that I believed it would only put us further behind, since most of our competitors wouldn't demonstrate the same restraint."

Autry later told the media that while he opposed the changes and was apprehensive about the game's future, he had an obligation to the Angels' fans, players and sponsors to do everything he could to produce a winner. It was an idea whose time had definitely come, since there had been periods when Autry seemed remiss in that obligation—remiss in regard to his farm system, to putting profits back into the organization, to keeping a close eye on the operation of his franchise.

Autry authorized the spending of $4 million and told Dalton he was particularly interested in Oakland outfielder Joe Rudi, considered one of baseball's best clutch hitters and defensive players.

The draft was held in mid-November, and Dalton then flew to Providence, Rhode Island, where he met with attorney Jerry Kapstein, who represented the players Dalton most coveted. What followed was a spending spree that made the $2 million Autry and partners had spent on 30 players in the 1961 expansion draft seem like a pittance.

Dalton and Kapstein first agreed on a contract for former Baltimore and Oakland outfielder Don Baylor, a power hitter who had never put a full season together and whose arm made him a liability in the field. If it were not for those limitations, Baylor might have done quite well in this auction. As it was, he received only $580,000 as a signing bonus and a six-year contract calling for a salary of $150,000 in 1977, $160,000 in 1978, 1979 and 1980, $170,000 in 1981 and $220,000 in 1982. The Angels also agreed to reward Kapstein with $75,000.

The signing of Rudi was announced the next day. Rudi received a signing bonus of $1 million and a five-year contract calling for a salary of $200,000 in 1977, 1978 and 1979, $240,000 in 1980 and $250,000 in 1981. The Angels paid Kapstein $100,000.

Dalton thought he was through at this point and packed to head home, happy with the additions of Rudi and Baylor. But before he could call for the bellman, another Kapstein client, Baltimore's All-Star second baseman, Bobby Grich, contacted his attorney.

Grich had been driving through New Mexico en route to his home in Long Beach, California, when he heard a radio report dealing with the Angels' largesse and decided it would be very nice to play for what he considered his hometown team. Grich found the nearest pay phone and called Kapstein, who called Dalton, who called Patterson, who snared Autry just before he walked into the press conference where the signing of Rudi was to be announced.

"Are you willing to spend a few dollars more?" Patterson asked.

"What's a few?" Autry replied.

"About a million and a half," Patterson said.

"Sure," Autry said. "I can always hock the saddle."

Patterson called Dalton, who initiated negotiations consummated 24 hours later.

Grich received a signing bonus of $600,000 and a five-year contract calling for $200,000 in 1977, 1978 and 1979, $240,000 in 1980 and $250,000 in 1981. Kapstein received $100,000, meaning that in three days the Angels had paid the attorney $275,000 for helping them sign three of his clients for approximately $5.2 million.

It was a high price for publicity, but the Angels now dominated the headlines, spurring an increase in the sale of season tickets from 3,718 to 5,879, helping defray the suddenly inflated budget.

Las Vegas responded by installing the Angels as an 8–5 favorite in the American League West. Manager Sherry responded to the rampant optimism by expressing a need for caution, saying the Angels still had to do it on the field.

His was now a set lineup, the most attractive in the club's history. Nolan Ryan reflected on the anticipated improvements in the offense and said, "I don't expect to have to go out there anymore with the feeling that every pitch is life and death, that with every pitch the game is in the balance."

The easygoing Sherry, a former Dodgers catcher credited with the recommendations enabling Sandy Koufax to shed the control problems that plagued his early years, knew the Angels still were not without questions. He knew it was still a game of pitching, and there was a question as to how much pitching the Angels had after Ryan and Tanana.

A number of people close to the club could not believe Dalton had spent $5.2 million of Autry's money on three offensive players, totally disregarding the club's pitching needs, particularly in the bullpen. The Angels made no attempt to sign Rollie Fingers, the game's premier relief pitcher, a Kapstein client who had been available in the reentry draft.

Dalton also made no attempt to improve the bullpen through trade. Dick Drago, Mickey Scott, Don Kirkwood and Sid Monge, who had combined for a 22-27 record and just 9 saves in 1976, returned to form the heart of the arson squad.

It was not until May 11, 1977, with the Angels already four

games under .500 and the team ERA over 4.00, that Dalton responded, knowing that by then the other clubs would put a gun to his head as he talked trade.

He eventually assembled a hefty package of Bruce Bochte, Sid Monge and $250,000, dispatching it to Cleveland for relief pitcher Dave LaRoche. This was the same LaRoche he had traded to Minnesota in 1972 for the inept shortstop, Leo Cardenas. Dalton, it will be recalled, said at the time, "It is much easier to develop a relief pitcher than a shortstop."

The reacquired LaRoche responded with 13 saves and 6 wins, but it was again a season in which there were problems in addition to pitching.

Tragedy had again visited the Angels in January. Mike Miley, a 23-year-old former Louisiana State University quarterback, who was expected to fill a reserve role with the Angels en route to becoming the future shortstop, was killed in an auto accident near his Louisiana home.

Then, on Valentine's Day, lifting an air-conditioning unit at his new apartment in Long Beach, Bobby Grich felt a pain in his lower back. The doctors called it a herniated disc. Grich spent three weeks of spring training in traction, losing a chance to prepare for a season in which the pressure of their new contracts would weigh on each of the free agents and in which Grich, a four-time Gold Glove winner at second base, would move to shortstop, leaving second to Jerry Remy.

None of it seemed to matter on opening night when the Angels helped the new Seattle Mariners open the Kingdome before an SRO crowd of 57,762, a partisan assembly that saw Joe Rudi drive in five runs and Frank Tanana pitch a 7–0 shutout.

The Angels won three of the five games in Seattle, but then went to Oakland and lost four straight to the once-proud As, whose championship team had been decimated by free agent defections.

Rudi drove in 27 runs to tie the American League's April record, but Baylor, used primarily as the designated hitter, a position he detested initially because it demeaned his conviction that he was an all-around player, struggled through the early weeks, compounding the frequent absence of Grich and the inconsistency of the pitching.

Baylor, who would hit 16 homers and bat .281 during the second half, hit just .223 with 9 homers during the first, creating a new kind of pressure, that of fan abuse. The heat became so intense that the personable Baylor, who won the respect and admiration of the media by retaining his accessible and frank posture, was forced to provide his wife and son with security when they attended the games at Anaheim Stadium.

The touted Angels hovered at or near .500 through April and May, unable to generate momentum. Then the disintegration that characterized previous summers began.

Grich, batting .243 with only 7 homers and 23 RBI, made his last start on June 8 and underwent back surgery on July 3.

Rudi, batting .264 with 13 homers and 53 RBI, attempted to ward off a fast ball thrown by Nelson Briles of the Texas Rangers on June 26 and broke his right hand. Rudi did not make another start and underwent surgery on September 2.

Dalton attempted to repair the pitching wounds with cosmetic surgery in mid-June, acquiring Gary Nolan from Cincinnati and Ken Brett from the Chicago White Sox. Nolan reported with a sore arm and lost all three of his decisions with the Angels. Brett lost 10, but at least won 7.

On July 11, with the Angels 39-42 and 9½ games out of first place, Dalton made his annual managerial change, firing Sherry and replacing him with coach Dave Garcia, an anonymous veteran of more than 35 years in the game, 15 as a minor league player and 14 as a minor league manager.

Dalton had fired Dick Williams a year earlier because he was too overbearing. Sherry was fired because Dalton believed he was too much the other way. The Angels, he said, were flat, listless and "not fully motivated." He also said that Garcia, whose personality seemed to be strikingly similar to Sherry's, had the capability to be more direct and assertive.

Sherry, under whom the Angels were 76-71 overall, said he had been made a scapegoat.

"I felt I had done all I could do and that it wasn't my fault," he said. "We had been unable to use either Rudi or Grich and we hadn't been getting help from Baylor. You take those three guys away and you have pretty much the same team you had last year."

Second baseman Jerry Remy, whom Sherry had appointed

captain, concurred, saying, "It never changes. The manager gets blamed for the shortcomings of the players and the mistakes of the front office."

Garcia was Dalton's fifth manager in five and half years, and he said, "No one will ever have to worry about firing me. I'll be the first to know when I'm not doing a good job and I'll quit."

The firing of Sherry was accompanied by the firing of pitching coach Billy Muffett and the hiring of Frank Robinson, who had been fired as Cleveland's manager earlier in the season.

Robinson was hired as batting instructor, the decision to reemploy him stimulated by the belief that Robinson could be activated as a designated hitter if the Angels became involved in a pennant race, an eventuality that did not occur.

Garcia's Angels were 35-46, finishing fifth with an overall record of 74-88, and 28 games behind Kansas City.

The best numbers again belonged to Ryan and Tanana, in addition to Bobby Bonds, who returned from his hand injury to set a club record with 115 RBI. He also stole 41 bases and slugged 37 homers, tying a club record Leon Wagner had set in 1962.

Ryan missed three starts with leg injuries, pitched hurt in four others and still completed 22 of 37 assignments, fashioning a 19-16 record and an impressive ERA of 2.77. He struck out 341 batters in 299 innings, walked 204 and created a midseason controversy when he refused to accept an appointment to the All-Star game.

American League manager Billy Martin selected Ryan only after Tanana, one of Martin's original choices, had bowed out because of an injury. Ryan's pride was injured by the fact he was not chosen initially and he said he would spend the All-Star break at the beach, as he had planned.

Martin responded by saying, "I'll never again pick Ryan, even if he has 40 wins by the All-Star break."

Tanana approached the 1977 All-Star break as baseball's best pitcher, a swaggering and free-spirited southpaw who combined overpowering stuff with a knowledge of his art that seemed beyond his experience.

The Angels had signed Tanana to a five-year, $1 million contract (not including $600,000 in deferred money and

$50,000 to agent Tony Attanasio) before the start of the 1977 season, and he made it look like a bargain.

He was 10-2 with a 1.84 ERA at midseason, and he was in the process of pitching 14 straight complete games, a remarkable but debilitating streak that brought on an inflamed triceps tendon, the injury that took him out of the All-Star game and left him an irregular starter over the second half of the season.

Tanana did not work again after September 9, completing the year with a 15-9 record and the league's lowest ERA of 2.54. He was only 24 but he had already pitched 1,081 innings. And he was already beginning to pay a price, the tendon injury being the first of several he would suffer in quick succession, his physical skills eroding at the height of his career, forcing Tanana to become a finesse pitcher long before he had envisioned making that change.

There were several factors, including a designated hitter rule that kept starting pitchers in the game longer; a string of managers whose insecurity was such they were only interested in protecting their jobs; a failure by Dalton to strengthen the relief pitching and provide his managers with reason and confidence to lift Tanana earlier; a consistent unwillingness to shift from the four-man rotation Ryan favored to the five-man rotation favored by Tanana.

The two aces of the Angels' staff were not close, despite having lockers only a few feet apart in the Anaheim Stadium clubhouse. A difference in lifestyles was compounded by the sharp difference in regard to which rotation best served their and the club's needs.

When Tanana reacted to his 1977 injury by saying it was the result of a four-man rotation, Ryan said, "As far as I'm concerned, he hasn't pushed himself since the All-Star break. There is more to pitching than just going out there every four or five days and throwing a baseball. You have to prepare yourself mentally and physically."

Tanana responded to that criticism by saying the value of a five-man rotation in the face of a long season had been proven by other clubs, and it was time the Angels stopped "glorifying" their two-man staff, stopped giving in to Ryan's whims and desires.

"In the overall picture," Tanana said, having been asked if

coexistence was still possible, "it doesn't matter who does or doesn't get along. He'll do his job and I'll do mine. That's all I really want to say. I'm of the opinion that if you don't have something good to say about someone, don't say anything."

There was little good being said about the 1977 season, which ended with the Yankees, who had also invested significantly in the free agent market, defeating the Dodgers in the World Series to prove they were "The Best Team Money Can Buy."

The Great Expectations had again turned to frustration for the Angels. Autry's $5.2 million purchased him his "most disappointing season yet." There was even a lack of satisfaction, of solace, when he reflected on a club record attendance of 1,432,633. Autry found it difficult equating the record with a loss of $600,000.

He could see how the increased payroll was part of it, how the attendance increase compensated some for the amortized bonuses and salaries. But he was still too much of a businessman to understand and accept a $600,000 loss in a season of record attendance.

Autry met with Dalton late in the season and said he was distressed by seemingly unchecked expenses and the distribution of $300,000 in complimentary tickets, mostly through youth programs initiated by Patterson at Autry's urging when Patterson was hired as president.

Autry said he was considering the hiring of Emil (Buzzie) Bavasi, as a finance director. Dalton said he had no objections but didn't think there was room for both Bavasi and himself in the baseball department.

Autry assured him that Bavasi wouldn't interfere, and Dalton said, "It's your club and your money. You're entitled to hire anyone you want."

Autry had admired the gregarious Bavasi for many years. He had offered him Fred Haney's position as general manager when the Angels moved to Anaheim in 1966. Bavasi, still general manager of the Dodgers at that time and looking for a situation in which he could gain some measure of stock control, rejected Autry's bid. There was no other offer from Autry until he invited Bavasi to lunch in October of 1977.

Bavasi had resigned as president of the San Diego Padres a month earlier. He was 61 and ready to retire to his ocean view home in LaJolla, not far from San Diego. "I had no desire and no intention to return to a full-time position," he said, reflecting on his emotions as he met with Autry at Mr. Stox, a restaurant not far from Anaheim Stadium.

Autry, who had outlined his thinking in several telephone conversations with Bavasi, again explained that the club's financial situation had to be corrected, controlled, streamlined. He invited Bavasi to join the Angels as a chief operating officer, a finance director of sorts.

Dalton, Autry said, would remain in charge of player personnel. Patterson would forfeit his title as president (which chairman of the board Autry would assume) but retain his role as a community liaison and unofficial director of promotions and public relations.

It seemed improbable that the Angels or any organization could function smoothly with three men of the ambition and ego of Bavasi, Patterson and Dalton sharing power and responsibility, but Bavasi decided to accept the challenge. He went back to work under a complicated formula via which the bulk of his salary stems from bonuses for increased attendance and decreased expenses. And it was not long before people were saying that the E in Emil stood for Economy.

"I found the Angels to be a country club moneywise," Bavasi said. "I told Dalton I wasn't going to tell him what player to get or how to go about it, but I was going to have control over the finances, and all departments would have to come to me before they spent anything."

Patterson considered quitting. He had worked with Bavasi in the front office of the Dodgers and felt he could get along with him on a personal basis. However, he was hurt by the reduction in power (Patterson emerged as assistant to the chairman of the board), since he believed it was unjustified. Attendance had risen approximately 500,000 in his three years as president. No other club executive had ever made as many speeches or established comparable visibility in the community. Patterson had become president of the Anaheim Chamber of Commerce and co-chairman of the National Conference of Christians and Jews. The walls of his office were lined with plaques honoring him for his participation in various charity drives. He had begun to help make the Angels competitive with the Dodgers at the gate and on the sports pages. And now he was no longer president, no longer in charge of the administrative purse strings, no longer permitted to stimulate the growth of future fans via complimentary tickets to Little Leagues and straight-A students.

Bavasi reached an agreement with the city through which the Angels paid a service charge (46 cents in 1980) for each person entering the stadium, even those carrying complimentary tickets. This put an additional crimp into Patterson's programs and also prompted Bavasi to stop the distribution of complimentary season tickets to the media. Bavasi also studied the list of people allowed to eat pregame meals in the club's press room and reduced it significantly. The press room bar, which previously stayed open until the last person left, was now closed 45 minutes after the final out, or before most writers had finished their stories.

Patterson didn't like any of it, but he decided to stay, to resist the temptation to look elsewhere. It was a decision based on his age (68 when Bavasi was hired), his salary (which remained intact through Bavasi's first year and was then reduced), his affection for where he was and what he was doing, his conviction that, despite reduced power, he could still make contributions.

Dalton reached a decision of another nature. Bavasi informed him that $400,000 would have to be trimmed from the player development budget, and Dalton knew what that meant —the firing of scouts (the staff went from 21 to 12 during Bavasi's first year) and the signing of fewer high school and college free agents. He knew it meant that he would now be unable to do the job he had set out to do.

"As far as I was concerned," Dalton said, "Bavasi was now trimming muscle instead of fat. I didn't see any way of accomplishing our goals if player development was going to be curtailed. The timing was particularly bad because we were starting to make some real progress. It wasn't all at the top yet, all at the major league level for Gene to see, but it was definitely there."

As of 1980, Dalton's six-year tenure with the Angels had produced proven major league players in Carney Lansford, Willie Aikens, Ken Landreaux, Julio Cruz, Dave Collins, Bruce Bochte and Dave Chalk. Both Cruz and Collins were left unprotected ("The Angels must have protected the secretaries," a disbelieving Collins said at the time) in the 1977 expansion draft and established their reputations with other teams. Bochte became one of the league's best hitters after he was traded away. A few other Dalton products made it on a fringe basis. A few others still had a chance, something Dalton didn't believe he had with Bavasi controlling purse strings.

Dalton had two years left on a contract that had been extended twice. He didn't like the thought of leaving a job unfinished, of leaving with a 444-520 record and the knowledge many people would remember only that he had employed five managers, but he liked less the thought of staying amid restricted circumstances.

It was early November and he was thinking of placing himself in the job market when he received a call saving him the trouble. Milwaukee Brewers owner Bud Selig, having recently fired Jim Baumer as his general manager, sensed in the Angels' hiring of Bavasi the possibility that Dalton would be available. He had called Autry and received permission to talk with Dalton. The negotiations were brief. Dalton was offered a six-year contract and explained to Autry he couldn't refuse the money or tenure. Autry, satisfied with the Bavasi budget, made no effort to retain the man whose initial attractiveness had led the Angels' owner to risk a tampering fine.

Dalton became executive vice president and general manager of the Brewers. Bavasi, who a month earlier had expressed no real desire to return to a full-time position, became executive vice president of the Angels.

Then the economy move took a strange turn.

Chapter
XV

WHILE ENFORCING the new farm controls, Bavasi paused long enough to sign free agent outfielder Lyman Bostock for $2.2 million. Bostock had batted .323 and .336 in his last two seasons at Minnesota and came to the Angels via the recommendation of his Minnesota manager, Gene Mauch.

"Gene told me that Bostock was the second best hitter in the American League," owner Autry said, "and that he'd definitely win a batting title someday."

Bostock would have won it in 1977 except that his Minnesota teammate, Rod Carew, the American League's best hitter in the estimation of Mauch and most others, batted .388.

Autry, of course, was hungering for a winner, his appetite growing by the year. The $5.2 million he had spent in 1976 had not achieved the anticipated results—artistically, at least— but he was anxious to believe he was getting close, one player, maybe two, away.

Bostock was signed for a deferred bonus of $250,000 and a

five-year contract calling for $400,000 per year. He had be-
come available because of Minnesota's inability and unwillingness to offer him a similar package. The Twins, knowing
Bostock would leave at the end of the 1977 season, had cut his
salary 20%, which is the maximum allowed by baseball's Basic
Agreement. The man who would be paid $400,000 by the An-
gels was paid only $20,000 by the Twins.

Bavasi's ensuing decision to trade Bobby Bonds, his home
run and RBI leader, was a concession to the game's new economics.

Bonds had earned $180,000 in the final year of a two-year
contract and was committed to the Angels in 1978 via the
option year of that contract. The Angels knew that if they
didn't satisfy his desire for a new multiyear, multimillion-dol-
lar contract he could opt for free agency at the end of the
season, leaving the Angels with nothing in return.

Bavasi decided to act before that happened. He was also
motivated by the knowledge that Bonds had hit many of his
homers in less than pivotal situations and that his defensive
skills had slipped significantly.

In a trade roasted by the club's fans, but a trade beneficial
to the Angels, Bavasi sent Bonds and two promising youngsters, outfielder Thad Bosley and pitcher Dick Dotson ("A
future Tom Seaver," the Angels had said when signing him a
year earlier), to the White Sox for two pitchers with a combined major league record of 13-8 and a catcher who had experienced elbow and shoulder injuries while performing as a
reserve during most of the 1977 season.

The catcher, Brian Downing, eventually became a catalyst
in the Angels' pennant drive of 1979. So did one of the pitchers, Dave Frost. The other, Chris Knapp, won 13 games in
1978, then suffered a back injury detrimental to his future
success.

Bonds, who said Bavasi had no intention of signing him,
was not signed by the White Sox either. He was traded from
Chicago to Texas to Cleveland to St. Louis, extending a
strange odyssey that found him playing for seven teams in
eight years.

The trade in which he left Anaheim was recommended by

special-assignment scout Frank Lane, a former major league general manager whose reputation had been that of a precocious trader. Lane was in his twilight years, having lost much of his vision. He would sit in the press box, a radio at his ear, the local announcer helping him identify the shadows on the field. The man he worked under with the Angels was new to the American League. Bavasi had spent his career in the National and was open to advice in his new assignment. Lane was among those who provided it, pushing for the package obtained in exchange for Bonds. He then also offered support of a trade consummated 24 hours later. At that point there was no way of telling how much dealing Bavasi would do if Lane's radio held up.

This time Bavasi sent team captain Jerry Remy to Boston for Don Aase, a pitcher with potential, and what was described as "other considerations." The "other considerations" translated to $75,000 in cash, which the Angels employed in signing Boston's free agent center fielder, Rick Miller, a defensive standout.

Miller received a three-year contract totaling $450,000, meaning Autry had now spent close to $8 million on five free agent acquisitions.

It still did not get Autry his pennant, though it helped move him a step closer than he had ever been.

The Angels finished second in 1978, winning a club record 87 games while losing 75 and finishing 5 back of the Kansas City Royals, who won their third straight title in the American League West and lost their third straight playoff to the Yankees.

It was a season of triumph and tragedy for the Angels, a season in which the free agent acquisitions helped attract club record attendance of 1,755,386 and helped produce club records for hits and average.

It was also a season in which the owner helped undermine the authority of his manager. Autry had done it first during the final days of the 1977 season when, during the course of an interview concerning the status of Dave Garcia, he innocently expressed a particular fondness for Kansas City manager Whitey Herzog, who had been the third base coach under Bobby Winkles and Dick Williams.

Autry did not say he was going to attempt to hire Herzog and did not say he was going to fire Garcia. But he did draw a $5,000 tampering fine from Commissioner Bowie Kuhn and did create the impression he wasn't satisfied with Garcia.

Any doubt was removed a few weeks later. Gene Mauch, still under contract in Minnesota but unhappy with owner Calvin Griffith's refusal to stop the exodus of key players by meeting their contract demands, told Autry he understood the Angels were considering a managerial change and wondered if he could discuss the position with him if he first received Griffith's approval.

Autry responded affirmatively, telling his staff he had to have a more dynamic leader and personality than Garcia, that he had to have a man who could compete for media attention with Dodgers manager Tom Lasorda, a renowned extrovert who bled Dodger blue and prayed to the great Dodger in the sky.

Autry and Mauch both called Griffith and received his permission to talk contract. "If Gene doesn't want to work here," Griffith said, "I see no sense in trying to keep him."

A stormy reaction by the Minnesota fans, already angered over the loss of a number of star players, changed Griffith's mind. He called Autry and said he could not let Mauch go without compensation. The Angels responded by giving Griffith a list of secondary players, from which he was invited to choose one or two. The Twins' owner was not satisfied. He said he would require a front-line player for a manager of Mauch's stature.

The Angels balked. "We have high regard for Mauch," Bavasi said, "but we are not going to tear up the team to get a manager. What sense would there be in trading for a manager when you would then have to turn around and trade for the type of players you just gave up?"

Mauch remained in Minnesota and Garcia remained in Anaheim, Bavasi conceding, "The situation should have been handled better. Dave should have been told if he was or wasn't coming back. The point is, he's going to spring training as our manager. Mr. Autry and I support him 100%. A lot of skeptics are going to be surprised."

Among the skeptics was Frank Tanana.

"The Angels more than told Garcia he wasn't in control,"
Tanana said, "that he was only a hole card. It's a crime.
They've created a sticky situation that has trouble written all
over it."

Garcia didn't agree. He didn't believe his authority had been
diminished or the pressure increased. There was no pressure,
he said, comparable with the pressure of being the teen-age
support for your mother and four sisters, no uncertainty comparable with ending a minor league season as the manager in
Oshkosh or Danville or Mayfield and not knowing where, or
even if, you would open the next. Dave Garcia was simply
happy to have the job, the opportunity.

"Managers have *won* and gotten fired so why worry?" he
said. "Pressure is for the manager who walks into the park
knowing his club doesn't have a chance. I'm lucky. I don't
have that pressure. My club can win and I'm not afraid to say
it. I don't see why we can't beat anyone in our division. I
really feel we might win a hundred games. On a position-by-
position basis, I think we're better than Kansas City or
Texas."

Garcia didn't really get a chance to prove it. He was fired
on June 1, 1978, with his team four games over .500 and only
1½ games out of first place.

He was fired despite a protracted slump that prompted Bostock to donate his April salary to a Los Angeles church after
Autry refused his request not to be paid.

"We wouldn't give him a raise if he had a good month,"
Autry said, "so I'm not going to withhold his pay just because
he had a bad one."

Bostock opened the season with 1 hit in his first 23 at-bats
and 2 in his first 39. His frustration was so intense he began
hallucinating at the plate; so intense there were days he drove
to the stadium and simply sat in his car, unwilling to venture
inside until talked in by teammates; so intense that the man
known as Abdul Jibber-Jabber because of his constant chatter
became a virtual mute.

Bostock was hitting 127 points below his 1977 average when
Garcia was fired, and he said, "I'm the one who should go."

A calf injury caused Rudi, coming back from his broken
hand, to miss 22 of the first 41 games and drive in just 6 runs

through June 1; a hamstring injury took Ryan out of the rotation for three weeks; Grich, who batted .216 in April and May, was undergoing a prolonged struggle to regain his timing in the wake of back surgery; a case of nerves affected the new shortstop, rookie Rance Mulliniks.

The 22-year-old Mulliniks played erratically in the field and had only 5 hits in his first 46 at-bats, forcing Garcia to bench him. Dave Chalk was moved from third base to shortstop, opening third for another rookie, Carney Lansford.

Lansford had a season of the type expected from Mulliniks, but Garcia was not there long enough to enjoy it, his firing having been almost preordained.

Bavasi set the stage by second-guessing a series of Garcia's strategic moves and by asking Baylor to take a stronger leadership role.

A seven-game losing streak capped by a 17–2 loss to the White Sox on May 31 provided Autry and Bavasi with their final stimulus. Autry, listening to that game on radio in Palm Springs, some 1,500 miles from the action, heard announcers Dick Enberg and Don Drysdale question Garcia's failure to leave the dugout and argue with the umpires over a debatable decision, enforcing the owner's belief that a more aggressive leader was required.

Autry called Bavasi and suggested the hiring of a man he had once thought would become player-manager of the Angels, a man Autry had always been fond of, the former shortstop Jim Fregosi.

"I didn't know Jimmy that well myself," Bavasi said, "but I knew Gene admired him and I knew of a lot of baseball people who were high on his knowledge and aggressiveness. The funny thing is, the day Gene invited me to lunch at Mr. Stox, Jimmy was also there, having lunch at another table. And on his way out, he stopped and said, 'If you ever think about a managerial change, keep me in mind.' "

Bavasi responded to that thought soon after he was hired, calling the Pittsburgh Pirates, with whom Fregosi was a utility player, and asking their permission to talk with Fregosi regarding the managerial position at Salt Lake City, site of the Angels' triple A farm club.

It had long been Autry's belief that Fregosi would someday

become the manager. Salt Lake City seemed the perfect stepping-stone, since it would put Fregosi in the wings while Autry
fulfilled his contractual obligation to Garcia.

The Pirates, however, rejected the Angels' request, on the
basis that Fregosi was an important adjunct to their bench and
spirit (he once responded to a week of regular employment by
telling the Pirates, "Bench me or trade me"). The Pittsburgh
decision did not disappoint Fregosi, who said later he would
have refused the Angels' offer because "I didn't feel I had to
go to the minors to manage in the majors. I had already spent
two seasons managing in the Puerto Rican Winter League, and
that was comparable to managing in triple A. Bill Rigney had
always advised me to continue playing as long as I could. It
was his belief that I could gain as much experience playing,
listening and watching at the major league level as by managing in the minors."

It was different when Bavasi called again on the first day of
June. The Pirates said they couldn't stand in the way of Fregosi's opportunity to manage in the majors, and Fregosi said
he had now played long enough, that he couldn't reject a major
league offer, particularly from the team with which he spent
ten seasons.

"In my heart," he would say later, "the Angels have always
been my organization."

Fregosi thought about that when Bavasi's call reached him
in Cincinnati. It was an off day and the Pirates had scheduled
a team party, putting Fregosi in charge. He had just delivered
the ribs and beer, in fact, when he was summoned to the
phone.

Here was a man who had once played 952 of the Angels' 972
games in a six-year span, playing hard and then leaving it
behind him. He didn't brood into the night. He seldom missed
a party. He once said, "The title of my book will be 'The
Bases Were Loaded and So Was I.' "

This time he didn't get his first swallow. He bid adieu to his
now former teammates and left for the airport to catch a flight
for Los Angeles. He was baseball's youngest manager at 36,
having been preparing for more than a decade. He asked the
stewardess for stationery and reflected on some of the men for

whom he had played: Bill Rigney, Billy Martin, Chuck Tanner. He wrote down the qualities he most admired, the qualities he hoped to incorporate as manager of the Angels.

The plane landed and Fregosi tore up his notes.

"The hell with it," he said. "I'm just gonna be myself."

It proved to be enough, for in addition to an air of command, a sense of when and where to communicate, a feel for what he had done and how he had acted as a player, Fregosi represented the prodigal returned.

"When I got here," Don Baylor said, "pitchers did what they wanted to do, regulars did what they wanted to do. There was no control in the organization. In doubleheaders, pitchers would leave the park once they were taken out of the game. The first time it happened, Ryan said, 'That's the way we do it. That's part of it.' Jimmy said, 'No, that's not part of it. That's not the way we do it.' He stopped it right there.

"The players had been in charge and that was it. Dave [Garcia] wasn't a disciplinarian at all. Sherry wasn't either. Fregosi had been hired by Autry himself. We knew he was going to be around for a while. We knew he was going to be in charge."

Fregosi protected his authority by limiting its use. He asked his players only to show up on time and play hard. There were no rules pertaining to dress and curfew. He had few meetings, believing the more often you said the same thing, the more meaningless it became.

The relationship with Autry was a security blanket, the foundation of his authority.

"I think everybody feels he's more like a permanent fixture in the organization," Nolan Ryan said of Fregosi. "More than that, he's a product of the organization. He was very successful. He's very popular in the community. He's the first home-grown manager the organization ever had. He's not somebody else's reject."

Fregosi returned the slumping Rudi to the regular lineup and made Downing his regular catcher. Baylor, disgusted with his role as the designated hitter and desiring to be traded, was told by Fregosi that anyone who didn't want to stay would be accommodated. He was told he would DH, and DH a lot, if he stayed. They argued about it on the eve of the June 15 trading deadline and Baylor stayed, becoming Fregosi's designated leader, as well as designated hitter.

The Angels finished the season 62-54 under Fregosi, a pace comparable with that established under Garcia. They were in first place by a half-game on August 25, but were then swept in a three-game series at Boston, lost five in a row, and held on for second. The last month might have been different if Ryan (rib separation), Dave Frost (muscle spasms in the small of his back) and Ron Jackson (sprained wrist) hadn't spent most of it on the disabled list.

Ryan completed his injury-plagued season with a 10-13 record. Frank Tanana, 11-3 at one point, won only 7 of his last 16 decisions and finally conceded his arm was as sore as it had been the year before.

Dave LaRoche supplied 10 wins and 25 saves out of the bullpen, but there was no other relief, and no one to step into the rotation when Chris Knapp, 10-6 at the All-Star break and scheduled to pitch the first game of the second half, walked out in a contract dispute. He returned apologetically two weeks later, but the Angels had lost each of the three games he had been scheduled to start.

The offense, warming up for 1979, was the best in the club's history. Baylor was second in the league in homers (34) and fifth in RBI (99). Rudi came back from his wretched start to drive in 79 runs and hit 17 homers. Grich found himself in September, batting .356 for the month, to finish with a respectable .251. The unheralded Lansford led all American League rookies with a .294 batting average. Bostock regained his stroke and personality, batting .331 over the final four months to lead the Angels with a .296 average, a 149-point increase from his mid-May low of .147.

The resurgence might even have taken him to .300, since there were seven games remaining on the night of September 23, when Bostock left the team's Chicago hotel to visit with friends and relatives in Gary, Indiana. Even now, even after the investigation and two trials, details are hazy.

This much is important: Bostock was in a car driven by his uncle. Two female acquaintances were also in the car. A man police later identified as Leonard Smith, the estranged husband of one of the women, pursued the Bostock vehicle, overtaking it at a stop light. Smith got out of his car and fired a shotgun into the rear window of the Bostock car. Two people were hit. Smith's estranged wife suffered minor face wounds. Bostock was fatally wounded.

"I had a late dinner and got back to the hotel about midnight," Jim Fregosi recalled. "Ken Landreaux and Danny Goodwin were standing in front of the lobby. I was about to say that it was a little late to be going out when I noticed they were both in tears."

Another tragedy—the most devastating yet—had struck Gene Autry's team, claiming one of its most popular and talented players.

A series finale with Chicago the next afternoon was suddenly without meaning. The Angels dressed amid sounds of silence. The red-eyed manager sat in his office and said, "We're professionals and this is our business. We'll play this game like it should be played."

He breathed heavily and the tears came again. "Right now," Fregosi said, "the team has to be secondary. A man has lost his life. A good friend is gone. Lyman Bostock had a super feeling for the game. He was close to everyone. I'll hold a meeting, but there's not much I can say. Everyone knows what kind of guy he was."

The Angels won five of their last seven games, staving off mathematical elimination until the start of the season's last series. Fregosi called it a "show of character." Bostock's memory permeated the thoughts of both players and club officials. The best season in the organization's history suddenly carried new implications.

Bostock's $2.2 million contract was covered by an insurance policy with Lloyds of London. His widow, Yuovene, received the guaranteed provisions without financial loss to the Angels. The talent itself was uninsurable, seemingly irreplaceable.

"We're in a state of shock," Bavasi said. "We've suffered a physical and spiritual loss that will force us to restructure our entire thinking in regard to our needs. We had reached a point where we really needed only one other hitter, maybe one other pitcher. We didn't plan to go into the free agent market, and we didn't envision a major trade. Now we're looking at major needs again.''

The restructuring began in early December, 1978, with the purchase of Jim Barr, an irregular starter and relief pitcher whose seven-year record with the San Francisco Giants was a less than convincing 81-90. The Angels saw Barr as the right-handed complement to left-handed relief pitcher Dave La-Roche. Barr saw dollar signs. The free agent received a four-year contract calling for $150,000 a year, a $50,000 signing bonus, a $210,000 deferred commitment and a life insurance policy costing the Angels $150,000.

The next day Bavasi replaced Bostock with a close friend of the late outfielder, former Minnesota teammate Dan Ford, known as Disco Dan because (1) he had a financial interest in one and (2) he had a rhythm of his own. Ford's manager, Gene Mauch, definitely thought the talented player danced to his own beat, but it was again more a matter of contract that forced the Twins to make Ford available.

The anxious Angels, having already spent $9 million on free agents, agreed to a contract extension that allowed Ford to earn $200,000 a year for five years. The Twins accepted infielder Ron Jackson and catcher Dan Goodwin as compensation.

Goodwin, the Angels' No. 1 selection in the 1975 amateur draft, had received $100,000 when he signed out of Southern University. The Angels assigned him to El Paso and soon sent instructor Vern Hoscheit to look in on him. The young catcher had not thrown in a competitive situation for several months and was attempting to bring his arm along slowly. Hoscheit, a regimental assistant to Dick Williams, thought Goodwin was malingering and demanded he throw hard for nearly 20 minutes. Goodwin's arm was never the same and neither was the Angels' investment, though as a down payment on Ford he brought a dividend of another type.

Ford and Barr represented a mere prelude to the February acquisition of Minnesota's seven-time American League batting champion Rod Carew, who painted the Twins into a contractual corner and then received their permission to make his own deal.

It was a complicated situation. Carew, a .334 lifetime hitter who has won more batting titles than any player except Ty Cobb, Honus Wagner, Rogers Hornsby and Stan Musial, was scheduled to become a free agent after the 1979 season, during which the Twins would pay him $220,000, loose change compared with what he could make on the open market.

The Twins, having already suffered significant player losses because of their inability to cope with baseball's inflationary economics, knew they would be unable to satisfy Carew's contract demands and knew they would get nothing in return if he was allowed to play out his option with them in 1979.

They invited Carew to reach a contract agreement with the club of his choice, at which point the Twins would then attempt to consummate a trade with that club. The Panamanian didn't require urging, for in addition to the financial considerations, the last of his affection for the Twins had been destroyed when allegedly inebriated owner Calvin Griffith delivered a speech containing racial slurs while at a suburban Lions Club meeting.

Carew immediately looked toward Anaheim, expressing an interest in the laid-back lifestyle, the cleanliness of the ball park, the potential of the team and the size of the contracts the Angels had been handing out. The flattered Angels did not intend to disappoint the All-Star first baseman. Bavasi and his assistant, Mike Port, went to the airport to greet Carew and his attorney (brother-in-law Jerry Simon) on their arrival in Los Angeles. The four huddled at a nearby hotel and required only the one negotiating session. Carew agreed to a five-year contract for a basic $4 million before cost-of-living increases.

The announcement was made on January 18, 1979. It was not until February 3 that the Angels and Twins consummated the trade that officially brought Carew to Anaheim. And it wasn't easy. The Twins kept demanding third baseman Carney Lansford and the Angels kept telling them Lansford wasn't available. Carew turned to the Giants and Yankees. It seemed that the "Best Team Money Can Buy" was about to get even better. Then suddenly the Yankees withdrew their trade offer. Owner George Steinbrenner explained that critical remarks Carew had made regarding the fans and city of New York had made it clear he "doesn't understand the privilege of playing for the New York Yankees."

It was three weeks before the start of spring training, and the Twins were getting nervous. The Yankee withdrawal came as a surprise. They liked the New York proposition better than that of the Angels, but now, since Carew had said he would not go to the National League, they had only the Angels. Twins vice president Howard Fox called Bavasi early on the afternoon of February 3 and resumed negotiations, consummated several hours later.

The Angels agreed to give up outfielder Ken Landreaux, the Minor League Player of the Year in 1977; pitcher Paul Hartzell, pitcher Brad Havens and catcher Dave Engle. Both Havens and Engle had played only in the minors, and neither Hartzell nor Landreaux had yet proved themselves over more than one big league summer.

Autry might finally have to hock the saddle, but Bavasi had obtained Carew without parting with either a regular pitcher or player. There seemed to be prospects in the package delivered to Minnesota, but Angel prospects seemed seldom to fulfill their potential.

"We hate to give up young players," Bavasi said, "but with the addition of Carew we have a chance to win it all. Right now we can put eight real fine major leaguers out there, guys who can play. I think Carew is a winner. He knows what it is to play hard in September."

Carew paid off long before that. The announcement of his acquisition was made on a Saturday afternoon, and lines began forming at the Anaheim Stadium ticket windows almost at once. The offices, normally closed, were opened on Sunday. Season ticket sales jumped from 6,530 to 11,043. Season attendance jumped from a club record 1,755,386 to a club record 2,523,575 in 1979.

Fans rocked the Big A, which frequently in the past had resembled a mausoleum. The chant of "Yes We Can" became the theme as the Angels marched to their first title. The crowds' exhortations and the confidence of Jim Fregosi, who never wavered after predicting a pennant in the spring, helped the Angels overcome 47 injuries that forced Fregosi to use 81 lineups and helped overcome the ineffectiveness of a shell-shocked pitching staff that compiled an ERA of 4.34, highest in club history.

The Angels did it primarily with the most explosive attack in the major leagues. One hot hitter ignited another. There was an epidemic throughout the lineup as the Angels batted .282, which was 23 points higher than the previous club record, and scored 866 runs, an average of 5.5 per game.

Don Baylor won the American League's Most Valuable Player Award as he hammered 36 homers, drove in 139 runs, stole 22 bases and batted .296. The Angels' board of directors voted him a $100,000 bonus and the privilege of negotiating a contract extension, despite a club policy against it.

The disco craze even swept Anaheim Stadium, as Dan Ford drove in 101 runs, hit 21 homers and played right field in award-winning fashion, compensating on a statistical basis at least for the absence of Bostock.

Bobby Grich came all the way back from his back surgery, establishing career highs for homers (30) and RBI (101). Carney Lansford supported Bavasi's wisdom in refusing to trade him and stamped himself as the best player ever to emerge from the Angels' farm system, committing only 5 errors as he batted .287, hit 19 homers and drove in 79 runs. Another farm product from the Harry Dalton regime, Willie Aikens, spelled Rod Carew at first base some, was used some as a DH and responded with 81 RBI, 21 homers and a .280 batting average. Carew battled a hand injury but batted .318. Brian Downing altered his stance, lifted weights ("How come you're wearing your chest protector under your shirt?" Nolan Ryan asked when he saw the now muscular Downing for the first time), and compiled a .326 batting average, highest among the league's right-handed hitters.

The Angels were never behind by more than 4½ games and never ahead by more than 5. Kansas City, seeking its fourth straight division title, was 10½ games behind on July 19 and a half game ahead on August 31, when the Angels beat Cleveland, 9–8, to take a lead they did not relinquish.

Nine-eight was a characteristic score. The ferocity of the hitting and the inconsistency of the pitching were best illustrated during a pair of three-game series with Kansas City in July. The Royals swept the first, getting 45 hits and 27 runs. The Angels swept the second, getting 38 hits and 28 runs.

Any self-doubt the Angels harbored was erased during a mid-July series with the Yankees at Anaheim Stadium. Nolan Ryan pitched eight no-hit innings in the opener before emerging with a two-hit, 6–1, victory. The Angels fell behind, 6–0, early in the second game and were still trailing, 7–4, with two out in the ninth. The Yankees had relief star Rich Gossage on the mound when Lansford and Ford singled consecutively and Baylor homered off the left field foul pole for a sudden tie. Baylor then homered again in the 12th for a stunning win. The Angels trailed Cy Young Award winner Ron Guidry, 4–0, early in the series finale and were still down, 4–3, in the ninth when Bobby Grich hit a two-run homer for an equally stunning win and an improbable series sweep.

The hysterical crowd forced Grich to return from the clubhouse for a curtain call of the type that became habit over the second half of a season in which the Angels continually responded to predictions that they were on the verge of folding.

Critics examined the Angels' pitching staff and forecast an inevitable collapse. Nolan Ryan and Dave Frost each won 16 games, but there were long periods when both were unavailable because of injuries; Frank Tanana did not pitch between June 10 and September 4 because of his recurring arm injury and won only 7 games; Chris Knapp did not pitch between mid-June and mid-August because of a back injury and won only 5 games; five farm products summoned in emergency situations combined for only 4 wins; Dave LaRoche, the anticipated relief ace, compiled a 5.57 ERA while losing 11 of 18 decisions; and Mark Clear, the unanticipated relief ace, struggled through the second half, totaling 14 saves and 11 wins, 8 in the first half.

The August charge by Kansas City brought another from Don Baylor. He criticized Bavasi for a failure to respond to the pitching problems, suggesting to a reporter that Bavasi would rather let the pennant slip away than spend a few dollars on the required repairs. Bavasi responded by engaging the writer of the article, Jim Ruffalo of the *Orange County Register,* in a press box wrestling match. He then also purchased John Montague from Seattle, and Montague supplied significant help, winning two games and saving five during the final five weeks.

The key series of the final month started in Kansas City on September 17. The Angels were three games ahead when the four-game series began, and three games ahead when it ended.

Someone asked Jimmy Reese, the senior coach and senior citizen, about the pressure and how he was adjusting to it. "I've been able to take nourishment," he said.

The Royals won two of the first three games and were within two games of the lead when Autry fed the Angels some incentive before the finale. He sent Fregosi a tape recording of an interview between a Palm Springs radio station announcer and Kansas City owner Ewing Kauffman, in which Kauffman said he didn't care who won the American League West as long as it wasn't the Angels.

Kauffman's remarks stemmed from his conservative financial philosophy. The Royals seldom participated in the free agent auction, and Kauffman wasn't happy with those who did.

Fregosi played the tape in a locked clubhouse before the game, and the Angels then defeated the Royals, 11–6, to regain a three-game lead with nine to play.

The race ended five days later when the Angels officially eliminated the Royals, beating them, 4–1, at Anaheim Stadium as Tanana pitched a four-hitter, his virtuosity adding a Hollywood touch to the game that ended Autry's frustration and helped ease Tanana's.

The left-hander had returned to the Angels in early September after not being expected to pitch again in 1979. Keith Kleven, a Las Vegas physical therapist, had helped send Tanana back to work when some doubted he would ever work again. The crowds chanted, "Yes We Can," and Tanana proved he still could, proving it most dramatically in the game that clinched the division title, his first complete game since June 5.

"For us to win it and for me to pitch the clincher," he said, waving a bottle of champagne exultantly, "well, hell, it's unbelievable. I've never been this happy. It's like a script. It takes some of the sting out of all the BS I've had to go through this year, out of all the frustration of the last six years."

Tanana took a hearty swallow from his bottle and poured the rest over his head. He grabbed another and sprayed Autry, who paraded from player to player, beaming like a new father. The Angels had won their first title and the price didn't matter. The long wait was forgotten. The mistakes and misfortunes yielded to the satisfaction of the moment. The memory of the years when the Angels simply didn't have the talent was washed away by the domestic champagne.

"There's been more spirit on this club than any I've ever been associated with," Ryan said. "These guys never knew when to quit. We didn't have any real cheerleader types, but we had a lot of guys who wanted to win."

Bobby Grich had won before. He had experienced the feeling as a member of the Baltimore Orioles. This was different, he said. "This is a dream come true. I've been an Angels fan since I was a kid. I used to come out to this park when Fregosi and Knoop were playing. I'd sit in the stands and say, 'I'd like to be out there someday.' Now here I am. It's unbelievable."

The dream ended there. The bid to turn Autry's half pennant into a whole pennant failed. It was probably not surprising, since the Angels had left a measure of their emotion in that wet clubhouse. Also they entered the best-of-five playoff series with Baltimore at a disadvantage.

Willie Aikens had strained ligaments in his left knee during the September series in Kansas City and was unavailable. Hard luck Joe Rudi was still sidelined by a strained Achilles tendon suffered in mid-August. Jim Barr had broken his finger in an altercation during the division-clinching party.

The pitching-rich, fundamental-minded Orioles, a team whose strength, manager Earl Weaver said, was in its depth, took advantage of California mistakes to win the first two games in Baltimore: 6–3 on a 10th-inning homer by John Lowenstein and 9–8 when Don Stanhouse finally choked off an Angel rally that began with Baltimore leading 9–1.

The series moved to Anaheim, with the Angels encountering turbulence en route. Broadcaster Don Drysdale, a fierce competitor during his years as a standout pitcher with the Dodgers, accused Barr of malingering, saying he was capable of pitching despite what the doctors had said about his injured hand. Barr and Drysdale moved toward each other menacingly, but coach Bobby Knoop separated them before a punch was thrown. Manager Jim Fregosi now left his seat to join the argument, defending Barr and telling Drysdale to stay off his players. Hard words were exchanged, but no blows.

The plane landed without additional problems, and Drysdale called Fregosi the next morning to apologize. "I heard something I didn't like and I said something I shouldn't have," Drysdale said. "It shouldn't be misunderstood. We are all on edge. It was a momentary disagreement and I take full blame."

The Angels displayed some fight of their own that night, scoring two runs in the ninth for a 4–3 win in game 3, their only win of a series that ended in game 4 when Scott McGregor pitched a six-hit, 8–0, shutout.

The zealous fans brought the Angels out of the dugout for one final curtain call, the long and loud salute providing the team with a warm remembrance to carry through a winter that turned cold in a hurry.

Chapter
XVI

EVEN BEFORE the 1979 season had started, some three weeks before the first pitch of a summer that produced the Angels' first divisional championship, Nolan Ryan had predicted it would be his last with the Angels.

Ryan was approaching the final year of a three-year contract that called for a signing bonus of $200,000, a yearly salary of $250,000, a $20,000 payment each year for five years after the contract ended, and a $50,000 interest-free loan to be deducted from his salary and paid Ryan each January of the contract's life.

At the end of the 1978 season, through attorney Richard Moss, Ryan wrote a letter to Bavasi in which he said that if the Angels would like to extend his contract past the 1979 season, he would be receptive to negotiations. But, Moss wrote, if those negotiations were not consummated by the start of the season, Ryan would declare his free agency in October.

"The one thing I want to make clear," Ryan said in the spring of 1979, "is that I don't want to be distracted by trying to negotiate a contract during the season."

Bavasi responded to the letter by asking Moss and Ryan to submit a proposal in January, 1979. The proposal was for a four-year contract at $550,000 per year. Bavasi took it to Autry, who decided that since Ryan was 31 and coming off an injury-plagued, 10-13 season, the Angels should allow him to play out the year and then, perhaps, retain negotiating rights by selecting him in the reentry draft.

It was a cold and curious decision in that Autry seemed to be turning his back and bidding adieu to the most spectacular pitcher of the 1970s, a man whose drawing power was worth a minimum of 1.4 million fans during his seven years with the team, that is, 1.4 million above what the club would otherwise have drawn.

Ryan expressed disappointment. "The Angels don't owe me anything," he said, "but I do feel that I've given them everything I've got and that I have made contributions at the gate and on the field. I've been totally loyal, and I would expect the same from them. Buzzie has said he might be willing to look at the situation somewhere around the All-Star break, but that's unsatisfactory. I don't expect an offer and I don't expect my attitude to change."

It didn't. Ryan played out his contract, contributing 16 wins and 223 strikeouts to the championship summer, and then became baseball's first million-dollar-a-year pitcher, signing a four-year contract for $1.1 million a year with the Houston Astros, who play indoor baseball some 30 minutes from Ryan's home in Alvin, Texas.

A personality clash between Bavasi and attorney Moss marred the final, fragile attempts to keep Ryan in Anaheim. Bavasi's last offer was for the same amount Ryan had been seeking at the start of the year. By then, however, Ryan knew he could double it in the market, and his pride had been injured by the Angels' attitude.

"Buzzie tried to embarrass us," Moss said, "by saying we made a final proposal for a million a year. Hell, it was strictly a bargaining position. We sat and waited for a counterproposal and it never came. Buzzie still thinks this is the mid-fifties and he's the general manager of the Dodgers and the name of the game is trying to sign a player for $15,000 when he's been authorized by Walter [O'Malley] to give him $16,000. All the talk about Buzzie getting a piece of the action, I don't think that's what it's about. He has to win. He has to beat people.''

Plagued by wildness and inconsistent support, Ryan was 138-121 with the Angels. His departure, Bavasi said, did not represent a serious loss since "all I have to do is find two pitchers capable of going 8-7 each." It was an attempt at humor, a reference to Ryan's 16-14 record in his final season with the Angels.

Fregosi and his players didn't laugh. It wasn't Ryan's record they worried about replacing as much as his workhorse capability, his average of 250 innings per season. They worried about the injuries that had sidelined Chris Knapp and Frank Tanana in 1979, about the uncertain nature of the bullpen, about the suspect status of a staff that permitted almost 4.4 runs per game en route to a championship.

"We overpowered people last year," MVP Don Baylor said, "but that's not the way to build a club or to win consistently. You do it with pitching and defense, but I'm concerned again that our front office has been lulled to sleep by the success of last year and again won't respond to what are obvious needs."

Handicapped again by the shallow farm system, Bavasi did respond, but in a questionable manner.

He first spent another $2.4 million to sign Pittsburgh free agent Bruce Kison as a replacement for Ryan—a replacement in body only.

Kison averaged only 140 innings annually during his nine years with the Pirates, never winning more than 14 games in a season. His availability was often curtailed by hand and elbow injuries, and he would become unavailable to the Angels in midseason because of a nerve condition that required elbow and wrist surgery.

Bavasi responded to Kison's loss by saying he had been signed on the recommendation by Fregosi and pitching coach Larry Sherry, both formerly employed in Pittsburgh.

Kison received a $750,000 signing bonus, a deferred commitment of $800,000, a $15,000 relocation allowance and a five-year guaranteed contract for $160,000 per year.

Bavasi then went to baseball's winter meetings in Toronto and negotiated a trade that would have sent his expendable first baseman, Willie Aikens, to the New York Mets for Craig Swan, a pitcher of acknowledged ability, of the type the Angels desperately needed.

Bavasi and Joe McDonald, the Mets' general manager, shook hands on the deal, but New York owner Lorinda de-Roulet, on the verge of selling her club, decided it would be unfair to the new owners to make a trade of that magnitude. Bavasi, who was headed to the press room to make the announcement, described the Mets' withdrawal as "the worst thing that's ever happened to me in baseball."

The most significant ramification was that it seemed to affect the Angels' perception of their needs. Instead of continuing to use Aikens as the bait in a bid for pitching, Bavasi quickly rebounded from the loss of Swan to trade Aikens for Kansas City outfielder Al Cowens.

Bavasi's explanation was that the Angels also required outfield protection, since Joe Rudi was coming off his Achilles injury and Dan Ford had undergone postseason knee surgery. The Angels obtained Cowens on December 12, 1979. They traded him on May 28, 1980, securing Detroit's Jason Thompson, a left-handed-hitting first baseman like Aikens.

There were four months left on the schedule after the Thompson acquisition, but the season had already ended for the Angels, the bid to repeat as division champion wiped out by what Bavasi called the worst injury wave he had ever seen. At one point seven Angels were on the disabled list. Five, including Ford, underwent some form of surgery. Don Baylor, Dan Ford and Brian Downing, who had combined to hit 69 homers and drive in 315 runs in 1979, combined to hit 14 homers and drive in 102 runs in 1980. Baylor broke his wrist, and Downing his ankle. Ford never regained strength and confidence following knee surgery.

The decimation of the offense placed the burden on a pitching staff unable to shoulder it. The decimation of the pitching staff put the burden back on the decimated offense. The Angels scored 168 fewer runs than in 1979. The team ERA climbed to 4.52, a new club record. Kison won 3 games and Dave Frost 4. Of 10 pitchers on the opening-day roster, none had a winning record when the season ended.

The champion Angels fell to fifth, 31 games behind once again dominant Kansas City. The record was a disturbing 65-95, and it was accompanied by the inevitable displays of emotion.

Baylor and Tanana criticized the club's response to the pitching crises, and Baylor said the club had prepared for the season complacently. Tanana and LaRoche said Fregosi lacked confidence in them, and asked to be traded. Rod Carew, who was unfazed by the ruin around him and batted .331, stopped talking baseball with the press because, he said, his quotes were being twisted and used against him in what was tantamount to a lack of respect. Ford said that the obvious inability to repeat as division champions should have eliminated the need to push his knee by rushing him back to the lineup, prompting Bavasi to say, "Someone should give Ford a fat lip, and I would do it if I was twenty years younger."

There was also the inevitable pressure on Fregosi, a Manager of the Year candidate the year before. This time the second half was played amid rampant rumors of his imminent firing. Bill Rigney, Fregosi's former manager and tutor, who had returned to the organization as special assignment scout, raised eyebrows throughout the league by frequently second-guessing Fregosi, an attempt, some said, to create an atmosphere in which Rigney would be rehired as manager.

The disagreements with Bavasi over player personnel, the disagreements all managers and general managers experience, took on new importance. No longer did Fregosi appear to be Autry's "favorite son." The unhappy owner asked Bavasi to join the Angels in Detroit in August and use his own discretion in regard to Fregosi's future. Bavasi said he would be unjustified in firing Fregosi, since the injuries had made it impossible to tell what kind of team the Angels had. X-rays of Fregosi's abdomen disclosed that the manager had 18 inches of colon removed in a postseason operation. He also lost his pitching coach (Larry Sherry) and batting instructor (Deron Johnson), each fired in the front office's quest for scapegoats.

The long summer weighed heavily on Gene Autry, who was among those who had seen only the promise. He searched for solace in the fact he had not been alone. The allegedly knowledgeable oddsmakers had favored the Angels to repeat. The eager fans had purchased 17,514 season tickets, an American League record. Anaheim was alive and roaring, but there was a sense of betrayal in the Angels' performance. The memory of 1979 faded and the cheers turned to boos. The roars now came from Autry.

He spoke frequently about his disappointment and frustration. He blasted the players for their lethargic play and said the pitchers lacked guts. He said the smart thing would be to call up his Salt Lake City farm team as a full-scale replacement for the varsity. The frequency and intensity of his criticisms were uncharacteristic and seemed to stem from the disheartening loss of his wife, Ina, who died unexpectedly in May, 1980.

A little more than a year later, on July 19, 1981. Autry married Jacqueline Ellam, a Palm Springs banker. The marriage seemed to provide Autry with his only happy moments during a year in which the Angels again failed to fulfill expectations, and the season was interrupted for 50 days by a strike of the Major League Players Association.

The strike prompted baseball's owners to split the season in two, the first and second half winners meeting in a divisional playoff preceding the annual Championship Series that matches the division winners.

Not even two seasons were enough for the Angels, however. They were 31-29 in the first half and 20-30 in the second, when they were last in the West. Their overall record of 51-59 put them 13½ games behind Oakland, the division's overall leader.

It was a season in which the philosophies of executive vice president Buzzie Bavasi were questioned and criticized by his players, and a season in which Autry made his seventh managerial change in eleven years.

Jim Fregosi, the prodigal who had led the Angels to their

only ever championship less than a year and a half earlier, was
fired on May 28 with the Angels 22-25. He was replaced by
Gene Mauch, whom Autry had hired in January as director of
player personnel.

It was a move Autry had originally attempted to make in the
winter of 1977, when Mauch was manager of the Minnesota
Twins and Autry wanted him as a replacement for manager
Dave Garcia. Mauch wanted it, too, but Minnesota owner
Calvin Griffith said he would not allow Mauch out of his
multiyear contract unless the Angels compensated the Twins
with players. The clubs could not agree on the players, forcing
Mauch to remain in Minnesota and Autry to stay with Garcia,
who went into the season knowing his boss didn't want him
and knowing his players knew it, too.

Garcia was replaced in midseason by Fregosi, who would
enter the 1981 season under the same pressures and shadows
as his predecessor. Autry insisted that Mauch had been hired
only as a possible successor to Bavasi, hired to give the club
the benefit of a field man in the front office, but Fregosi suspected otherwise.

"I have to believe he was hired," Fregosi said following his
firing, "because Gene questioned my ability right from the
start."

Mauch, 55, had quit as Minnesota's manager in August of
the previous year. The frustration that led him to resign
stemmed from owner Griffith's refusal to stop his best players
from entering the free agent market, by offering them the lucrative contracts available elsewhere, and from a career spent
with losers.

While considered one of the game's top strategists, a trim,
tanned, silver-haired man who is dedicated to the game and
known as the Little General because of his military air, Mauch
had a 1,524-1,705 record when he resigned. In 21 seasons with
Philadelphia, Montreal and Minnesota, Mauch had never won
a title of any type, a string of failures that became a record 22
seasons with the Angels. Only Connie Mack, John McGraw,
Bucky Harris and Casey Stengel had lost more games than
Mauch, but all are in the Hall of Fame and together won 32
pennants and 17 World Series.

"I've had enough of building bad clubs," Mauch said at the time he quit in Minnesota. He also said he would never manage again, but he was soon tempering that, saying he would only manage in a winning environment, only with a club that had a chance to win.

When he accepted the front office invitation extended by Palm Springs neighbor Autry, Mauch said that "not for one instant am I thinking of managing the Angels. I have no designs on Jimmy's job. I have even asked Buzzie to include a clause in my contract that would prevent me from managing the club as long as Buzzie is here."

Bavasi refused, saying, "Things change."

Things did change, as the cynics thought they would and as Fregosi's intuition told him they would.

The pressures mounted as the Angels' touted offense got off to a sluggish start; Oakland won its first 11 games and 17 of its first 18; Bavasi played ill-advised mind games with Fregosi's designated hitter and clubhouse leader Don Baylor (once prompting Baylor to retire briefly); the press, responding to a series of damning statements from Autry and Bavasi, created an atmosphere of uncertainty surrounding Fregosi; and Autry delivered ultimatum after ultimatum, culminating in his firing of a man frequently portrayed as his surrogate son.

Of that pressure during Fregosi's final weeks, a veteran Angel said, "They've laid so much BS on Jimmy that he's now finally given up."

Fregosi waited several months before saying he would never work for Autry again. He said, "They brought me back as a 36-year-old man and treated me as if I was still the 17-year-old kid."

He also said, "The one thing I'll never understand is this: If the man wanted to fire me, why didn't he fire me? Why did he create a day-to-day situation in which he was too embarrassed to walk into my office and look me in the face and which made the conditions that much harder to work under? How could I walk into the clubhouse and kick a player's ass when he could say to me, 'Hey, what does it matter? You're not going to be here tomorrow anyway' ? I learned a lot and I now know I wouldn't work under those conditions again. I put enough pressure on myself without having to put up with people in my own organization putting it on me."

His firing, Fregosi contended justifiably, was an act of panic by a management that did not understand how Oakland's improbable start had led to a false imbalance in the West and did not understand that the Angels—with eight new pitchers (from opening day of 1980) and with a new shortstop, third baseman, left fielder, center fielder and catcher—needed more than 47 games to develop cohesiveness, faith in each other, and a belief that as a team they were as good as everyone said they were.

"I'm also not sure," Fregosi said, "it was recognized or accepted [by management] that when you build a team on hitting, you live when it hits and die when it doesn't. When you build a team on pitching and defense, you have a chance to win no matter what you score. You win with pitching, defense and speed. Hitting comes fourth. When we won in 1979 it was with [a comparatively low] 88 wins and with the hitters mashing the ball. Those things aren't going to happen every year. You can't expect hitters to have the best year of their careers every year."

Fregosi had repeatedly drawn Autry's criticism for failing to bunt more, to hit and run, to steal. He was expected to play for a run at a time, even though he didn't seem to have the kind of pitching that could win low-run games or the speed to allow him to play a running game. Mauch changed the style but not the substance. The lack of hitting put an obvious burden on the pitching and defense (the Angels led the league in errors). A frustrated Mauch held a September clubhouse meeting and said his players were quitters. The Angels responded by losing 14 of their next 15.

Fregosi, listening via radio and watching via television, cited a lack of front office direction and continuity. He said the pressure to win a pennant for "poor old Gene Autry" before he dies, coupled with Autry's belief in the star system, in a philosophy that you can buy a pennant, has prevented the Angels from "adopting a policy and sticking with it." He spoke from the experience of 14 years in the Autry organization.

"One year," he said, "they're building through the farm system, the next year it's with free agents. The Angels have never had the same six or seven [front office] people working together over the years for the same goals. They did have it for a while in the early years but weren't willing at that time to put their money in the farm system, to build a foundation."

The "win now" policy of the later years, Fregosi said, has compounded the inadequacies of the farm system and prompted the trading of the few farm products of proven ability—Ken Landreaux, Dave Collins, Carney Lansford, Willie Aikens, Jerry Remy and Julio Cruz among them. All except Collins were signed during Harry Dalton's tenure as general manager. Collins was signed by Dalton's predecessor, Dick Walsh.

"No championship club could have survived the injuries we had in 1980," Fregosi said, "and that was the year the inadequacies of the farm system really showed up. You've got to give your young players a chance to mature, but they had traded away a lot of the kids who seemed close to playing in the big leagues or had already proven they could.

"My goal when I came back was to win a championship, and we did that at least on a division level. We not only had to beat the other teams, but had to tear away the reputation of always having been a loser, of being a hard luck organization. No matter what happened to me later, I'll never forget the thrill of finally seeing that stadium filled, the look on the faces of the people who had been with the club for a long time when we finally won, and the positive reaction of the fans when we lost to Baltimore in the playoffs. You can live a lifetime and never be fortunate enough to experience any of that."

Mauch is still waiting. The problems that cost Fregosi his job remained under the new manager. A lineup that featured three former winners of the American League's MVP Award and six hitters who had driven in 100 or more runs in a season generated an average of just over four runs per game. The pitching was better than expected, but incapable of producing the occasional shutout or low-run game required to snap the Angels out of a slump.

The misfortune of previous summers was also evident again.

Center fielder Fred Lynn, considered one of the game's best all-around players, a player who had signed a four-year, $5.3 million contract following his winter acquisition in one of two major trades with Boston, batted only .219 (89 points below his career average) and underwent September surgery for a knee injured in May.

As the Angels played out a frayed string, several players criticized Bavasi for his attempt to build a pitching staff with quantity instead of quality. In the two years since he had refused to meet the contract demands of Nolan Ryan, Bavasi had spent $7 million on free agent pitchers Bruce Kison, Geoff Zahn, Bill Travers, John D'Acquisto and Jesse Jefferson.

While Ryan was winning 22 regular season games and pitching a fifth no-hitter for Houston, the five Angels were totaling only 19 wins, 10 by Zahn. Travers, given $1.5 million despite a history of arm troubles, developed tendinitis during spring training and pitched only 9⅔ innings for the Angels in 1981. D'Acquisto, given $1.3 million despite a career record of 34-50, was sent to the minors in May and did not return. Kison, given $2.4 million before the 1980 season (despite having never won more than 14 games in a season), won 7 games in two years and was out a full year while recovering from nerve surgery.

Bavasi responded to the criticism by saying the problem with his team in 1981 may have been that the players were trying to do two jobs—run the club and play ball. Autry, who had virtually underwritten the free agent system on his own, said he was through with that system, that the club would now build from within. He said bitterly that all the lucrative, long-term contracts seemed to have diluted some of his players' intensity and aggressiveness.

However, this philosophy suddenly reversed itself in late January 1982 when one of baseball's most spectacular, popular, and glamorous stars, Reggie Jackson of the New York Yankees, became a free agent and then was unable to resolve his contractual demands with the Yankees' controversial owner, George Steinbrenner. After weeks of sparring and tentative negotiations, Jackson was signed to a four-year contract with the Angels, largely because he was promised he would be the team's right fielder and be in the line-up regularly, whereas the Yankees had planned to use him essentially as the designated hitter. It was sad news for the host of Reggie-Yankee fans but intensely exciting news for Angel rooters, who saw in Reggie a true superstar who could lift the team out of the mire into which the Angels had sunk in 1981.

The heat of another disappointing summer passed, however, and the soft glow of autumn diminished the passions of the former American Legion shortstop from Tioga, Texas. Autry could now sit in his office at the Palm Springs hotel that carries his name and reflect on his 21 years as an owner in a more unemotional manner.

He could say that in the movies he hardly ever lost a fight and in baseball he hardly ever won one. He could say it had been the most exciting and frustrating experience of his life. He could say that much of the initial enchantment had ebbed but that he hadn't given up, that he was still an optimist, that no man would survive long in baseball if he wasn't.

And he could laugh heartily when it was suggested that the travails of the Angels could be summed up in the responses of one of the team's early relief pitchers when, while strolling on New York's Fifth Avenue with a young lady on his arm, he encountered his wife, who had flown in to surprise him.

"Well, honey," he said to the woman who wore his ring, "who are you going to believe? Me or your eyes?"

About the Author

ROSS NEWHAN is a native Californian, who was born in Los Angeles and raised in Long Beach. Attending Long Beach State College, majoring in journalism, Ross began working full time at the *Press Telegram* as a sports reporter.

In 1961 when the Los Angeles Angels franchise was created, Ross was assigned to cover the Angels. He remained in that capacity with the *Press,* until 1968 when he moved to the *Los Angeles Times,* covering both the Angels and the Los Angeles Dodgers.

Newhan has twice served as Chairman of the LA-Anaheim chapter of the Baseball Writers Association, and has received numerous writing awards. Newhan lives in Anaheim, Cal., with his wife Connie and two children, Sara and David.